Let's Eat Korean Food

LET'S EAT

KOREAN FOOD

HOLLYM
Elizabeth, NJ · SEOUL

First published in 1997
by Hollym International Corp.
18 Donald Place, Elizabeth, NJ. 07208, USA
Tel:(908)353-1655   Fax:(908)353-0255

Published simultaneously in Korea
by Hollym Corporation; Publishers
13-13 Kwanchol-dong, Chongno-gu
Seoul 110-111, Korea
Tel:(02)735-7551   Fax:(02)730-5149

ISBN 1-56591-071-0
LCC Card No.: 96-80013

Illustration© by Jin-duk Kim
Printed in Korea

CONTENTS

CONNOISSEUR'S CHOICE

CONTENTS

Introduction

Until recently Korea itself was not widely known to outsiders. And Korean food was not widely appreciated outside Korea's own boundaries. But today all that is changing.

More and more visitors are coming to Korea every year and many are interested in tasting the local cuisine. Very often they like what they taste. Then they are prepared to try Korean recipes in their own kitchens. And they are happy to try Korean restaurants set up by expatriate Koreans in their own home countries.

But the key to this burgeoning interest is taking the first step. A new cuisine can be a daunting prospect particularly if the language and the culture are totally new and a little difficult to penetrate. This book is designed to help the new visitor to understand Korean cooking and Korean restaurants.

It contains a comprehensive overview of Korea's main dishes, what they contain and how to select and enjoy a Korean restaurant meal. To help the newcomer still further, twenty or so specially starred selections have been included under the title of Connoisseur's Choice. These are tried and true dishes which are widely available and particularly well liked worldwide. If you know nothing about Korean cooking, you would be well advised to start here.

Armed with this book, you should be able to pilot yourself through a Korean menu with aplomb and thoroughly enjoy your visits to Korean restaurants. With this book in your hand, the national cuisine is open before you.

Go and try it. Go and enjoy.

Of courts and conquerors: the development of Korean cuisine

When you sit down to a Korean meal rice, a soup and a couple of dishes of pickled vegetable dishes will form the nucleus of your meal.

Rice is the most common of the cereal dishes on a Korean menu. It may be cooked alone or with other grains such as millet or barley, or with chestnuts and beans. Vegetables too may be mixed with the rice before serving. Rice gruel is also classed as a main dish and noodles and dumplings are sometimes substituted for plain rice to give festive occasions a celebratory twist.

Your meal will certainly have at least one bowl of *kimchi*. An essential component of any Korean meal, *kimchi* is a fermented pickle made from vegetables, commonly cabbage or radish, seasoned with red pepper, garlic, ginger, onion, salt, seafood and fish juice. After preparation it is stored to ferment in a stoneware crock.

Then you will be offered a range of smaller side dishes. They can be made from meats, seafood or vegetables or a combination of the three. They vary enormously in their saltiness and their spiciness and it is in the seasoning that the Korean cook displays her expertise.

The table spread before you may have many dishes or

just a few. Korean table settings are identified by the number of side dishes or *chops* which are served. They run from a simple 3-*chop* setting to a 12-*chop* table if the meal is a feast. The average family takes three side dishes at an everyday meal. If you are being entertained you will find many dishes, as the Koreans are generous hosts.

When you are eating, be prepared to dig into communal dishes. Some of the food may be served individually but there will be several dishes into which everyone digs with his chopsticks taking some choice mouthfuls onto their own plate.

A piece of fruit or a plate of rice cakes and cookies may signal the end of your meal but desserts are not essential at every meal occasion.

As for beverages, if you are eating at a family meal you will drink water or barley water, *bori cha*, with perhaps a fruit tea or punch at the end. But if your meal is a celebration or restaurant banquet you may be served alcoholic drinks.

The modern Korean diet owes much to the abundant harvests of the Korean peninsula and the seas around its shores. Seafood and seaweed are plentiful in the East Sea (Koreans never call it the Sea of Japan) and the Yellow Sea. Lowland areas of the country are rich in grain and vegetable production. Livestock is raised here too. On higher land farmers produce fruits and nuts while in mountain areas Korean cooks gather mushrooms and little known roots and greens.

These gifts of nature have been shaped by the ingenuity of Korean cooks down the ages. What you eat will be determined by the time of year and the region of the country in which you happen to be. Korean cooks always try to use seasonal products and local specialties.

But the diet has also been molded by influences from other parts of Asia, influences not always welcomed at the time, brought by invaders. Along with holy books and weapons of war came new food products and new ways of dealing with food that left an indelible mark on Korean domestic life. The Korean culinary folk memory goes back a long way.

An integral ingredient in Korea's modern diet, garlic, played an important part at the founding of the nation in 2333 BC. Koreans believe that their country came into being as a result of a union between a god and a bear. Legend relates that this happy coupling was helped along by twenty cloves of garlic. The bear begged to be made human and the god gave him the garlic and told him to go away for one hundred days. The animal reemerged a woman who then married the god. Their son, Tan'gun, was the founder of Korea. Ever afterwards the life-enhancing properties of garlic have been acknowledged by Koreans who eat it daily in almost every dish and in every form.

Documentary evidence of ancient Korean food production and cooking practices comes from Chinese and Japanese sources. The Chinese mention a Korean dish called *maekjok* which historians think may have been a forerunner to *pulgogi* and in the sixth century BC Korean bean fermenting skills are mentioned admiringly. 1300 years later, in 700 AD, a Japanese writer mentioned that fermented bean sauce or miso was introduced into Japan from Koryo (918-1392).

Animal husbandry has long been established in Korea. In Puyo, a walled city state, in the second century BC, great status attached to officials who were in charge of the Ox House, the Horse House, the Pig House and the Dog House. They ranked just below the king.

An important development which affected Korean food was the arrival of Buddhism from China around 400AD.

Increasingly, meat eating was abandoned in favor of a heavily vegetarian diet with some highly complex recipes. It was during this period, too, that tea began to be drunk and the dignified rituals of the tea ceremony evolved as an adjunct to Buddhist ceremonies. The creation of the tea pots and bowls needed for this ceremony contributed to the refinement of Korean pottery skills.

But the Buddhist influence did not go unchallenged. In the middle of the thirteenth century the Korean Koryo state was threatened by incursions from the Mongol tribes who had swept into China and Manchuria from central Asia. The Mongols eventually dominated the Koryo court completely and exacted tribute from a conquered population.

Among the items demanded as tribute were oxen which were raised by the Mongols on the island of Cheju-do. The rolling landscapes of this island off the tip of Korea were populated with large herds of cattle. From the Mongols Koreans learned the delights of cooked meat again. *Mandu* (dumplings) and *soju* (rice wine) were other additions to the Korean diet for which the Mongols were responsible.

Organized opposition to Buddhist culture came during the long Choson period (1392-1910) when the court espoused Confucianism. Diet again was affected. Tea drinking, for example, was discontinued in an attempt to strike at Buddhist ceremonies and practices. Boiled rice water was put in its place and only relatively recently has the practice of tea drinking been revived.

Boiled rice water, made in the pot in which the rice has been cooked and still containing a few rice grounds, may be worthy but, to some, it is not very exciting. So enterprising

individuals began to experiment and to produce their own rice wine. Modern *soju* is the result of those experiments.

It was in accordance with Confucian folklore that dogs began to be eaten again in Korea. They had been eaten before in both China and Korea but, during Confucius' life, had been the food of kings only. Korean Confucian scholars decided that they should be a part of the general Korean diet because they had been a delicacy in the lifetime of the philosopher. They are still eaten in Korea today. Confucian scholars also

encouraged the eating of raw food, including raw fish and raw meats, because of the master's example.

Other changes in Korean eating habits during the Confucian revival were the use of the spoon in addition to chopsticks at the table and the placing of food on altars and tables to worship the ancestors. This practice eventually produced the modern *pibimbap* dish. The ritual meats, vegetables and rice were put to good use after the ceremonies in this simple but tasty, mixed rice dish.

But the most revolutionary change in cooking during the Choson period came with the Japanese invasion at the end of the sixteenth century. After the end of hostilities the Japanese brought new fruits and vegetables such as red peppers, zucchini, sweet potatoes, corn and peanuts to Korea.

The impact of the red peppers cannot be over emphasized. Their color delighted the Koreans who believed it would ward off evil spirits. They experimented with the powder produced by grinding up the peppers. In 1766 red pepper powder was added to *kimchi* for the first time and its liberal addition to many dishes gives Korean food its

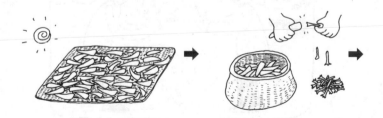

characteristic color and flavor to this day.

Many of the conventions of modern Korean cuisine have been handed down from the Court cuisine of the Yi dynasty which lasted until 1910. The king's food was cooked by special cooks who were recruited into royal service when they were about thirteen. They were usually girls from poor families who sent them to serve at court. There they were guaranteed lifetime's employment with all their living expenses met. Their sacrifice was that they were not allowed to marry.

The cooking these young women brought with them to the king's service was what they themselves had learned from their mothers. So royal cuisine was not so different from the cuisine of the common man though the seasoning was generally milder than everyday Korean fare. Royal food differed mainly in quantity, quality and care of preparation.

The common people ate whatever came to hand. Their diet was limited by what they could afford and what they could grow or produce for themselves. The court, however, enjoyed meals made from the best ingredients from every region regardless of cost or time. Every dish was prepared

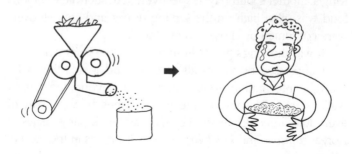

with an eye to aesthetics so that each fish or vegetable was arranged with care to appear as perfect as possible.

The portions at court were king-sized. In a culture where the luxury of a meal is judged by its complexity the number of side dishes or *chops* offered to the king in addition to the basic rice and *kimchi* and soup was always twelve. A poor man would count himself lucky to have three.

Dinner was a solitary affair for the king. He customarily dined alone attended by three female servants. One of them would explain to the king where the raw materials had come from for his meals so that the monarch could understand the specialties of each region at first hand. Another was responsible for tasting the food to guard against a poisoning attempt on his life. During the meal dancers and musicians would perform in the courtyard below his dining room and other guests would eat from individual tables at each side of this courtyard.

The cooks prepared special menus for celebrations such as birthdays or Chusok, the autumn harvest festival. On the king's birthday a special menu was written on red paper and sealed in a red envelope. Blue and yellow paper menus were the order of the day on the Queen's birthday and on the King's mother's birthday respectively. At such celebrations food was piled high on the serving dishes and any left-overs were consumed by chosen court officials.

It was the king's guests from the yangban class who were most impressed by the meals at court and it was they who brought information about court food beyond the palace walls. Gradually some of the court dishes became part of every Korean cook's repertoire. The two great party dishes of Korea, *shinsollo* and *kujolpan*, have their origins in the food of the Yi dynasty.

The modern Korean meal has a long history and a simple format but, within it, there is lots of room for variety. Read on.

A warm welcome: inside a Korean restaurant

You want to eat at an authentic local restaurant? An excellent idea. Korean cities, especially, abound in them. But you must be aware that there are one or two things which make them a little different from Western restaurants.

Korean restaurants are simple and functional. The service is brisk and to the point, without any airs and graces. But the people are gracious and are delighted to introduce you to their food and very appreciative if you compliment them on the meal they have provided.

Often you will be ushered into a large dining room with Western-style tables and chairs. But you may find that there are side rooms, or areas at the end of the dining room, which have a raised *ondol* floor. This is a floor which will be heated in the winter.

If you choose to eat in an *ondol* dining room you will find that the tables are low and you must sit on large flat cushions on the floor. This is pleasant on a cold day with the heat from the floor warming your legs but it can sometimes turn into an achingly uncomfortable experience for Western legs unused to sitting for a long period at this level. So, given the option, it might be better to choose the conventional seating until you are familiar with Korean ways.

There is another convention which must be followed in

ondol rooms. You are obliged to take off your shoes before you enter. Sometimes there is a shoe rack or cupboard by the door but often you simply leave your shoes on the lower level as you step up to enter. When you leave you will find your shoes have been reversed for you to step into them.

As you are getting yourself settled the waitress will bring you a welcoming cup of barley tea and a spoon and chopsticks. You will then be invited to order. Some restaurants have printed menus, occasionally with illustrations. In others the menu is printed and displayed on a wall.

Until you get adjusted to Korean food and Korean ways, a safe choice is *hanjongshik*, a table d'hôte menu of several dishes, which will come together with a bowl of rice and a dish of the national relish, *kimchi*, a pickled and fermented vegetable dish usually based on cabbage or radish.

On the table you will find pottery or stainless steel containers holding condiments. Salt and pepper will be there and probably also red pepper powder or paste, vinegar, mustard or soy sauce. Take care. Try your food before adding any of these. You will probably find it sufficiently seasoned without them.

Unlike a Western meal, in a Korean meal most of the dishes will come together. It is not as confusing as it sounds because it is all organized so that all diners can reach all dishes easily. In general rice and soup, the central dishes of any Korean meal, are immediately in front of the diner in the first row. In the second row are sauces. The third row is made up of cold dishes which are eaten with chopsticks on the left and warm dishes with broth which require a spoon on the right. The fourth row is arranged with vegetables on the left, *kimchis* in the middle and warm dishes without broth on the right. You select as your fancy takes you from any of the dishes and put the tidbits on your own plate.

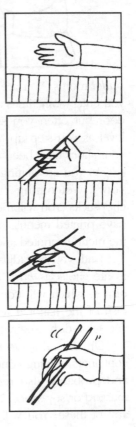

Metal chopsticks are used in most restaurants. They do need more practice than wooden ones. But getting acquainted with them does not take long if you follow a few simple rules. Hold your hand horizontally and parallel to the table with the palm facing you. Slip in your chopsticks and let them rest across your middle finger. Put your thumb across the chopsticks to hold them firm. You should then have the chopsticks one on top of the other.

Continue to hold the bottom one still and manipulate the upper one with your index finger and thumb to pick up your food. Try it a few times and you will soon be an expert.

There is less of a tradition of eating dessert at the end of a meal. If you have had an expensive *hanjongshik*, a veritable banquet, a piece of fruit will be served. A less sumptuous repast will not have a final sweet course.

You will probably drink barley or rice water with the meal if you do not have an alcoholic drink. At the end of the meal Korean fruit tea or punch may arrive. But do not expect Western tea or coffee. Koreans are much more likely to go out to a coffee shop nearby for a drink after the meal.

So the turnover of seats in the average Korean restaurant is quite quick and you may find yourself the object of irritation if you linger too long. If, however, you book a private room in a high class restaurant you will be

undisturbed for as long as you and your guests wish to stay.

Just a few final words of advice in case you are dining with Koreans. Follow these tips and you will be considered the perfect guest. Wait until the oldest person begins to eat before starting your meal. It is quite acceptable to chew food and to drink soup noisily but not to blow your nose while dining. Koreans eat mainly with chopsticks but rice and soup should be eaten with a spoon. During the meal leave your spoon and chopsticks, when not in use, on top of your bowl. When you have finished eating put them beside your plate. Another gesture you should make at the end of a meal is to pour a little barley water into the rice bowl. It shows your appreciation and makes the washing up a little easier.

Then there is that perennial problem, the bill. The person who has issued the invitation does the paying, usually at the cashier's desk beside the door. No tipping is required except occasionally at very high class establishments after a big party has been entertained.

Bear all these things in mind and you should enjoy your first restaurant meal. Soon you will be planning to do it again.

A touch of fire:
the seasonings of Korean food

You will soon realize that Koreans like their food hot. It is not the temperature. It is the spiciness that is palate busting. You will have come across some of the seasonings before. Vegetable oil, salt, mustard paste and vinegar, for example, are common throughout the world.

Sesame Seed oil   Vegetable oil   Vinegar   Mustard   Salt

But some well known ingredients are used in ways which give Korean food its unique flavor. Sesame seeds and soy beans, ginger and green onions and, perhaps best known of

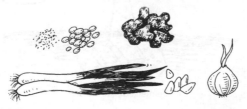

all, garlic are all flavors which are so much adopted in Korea that they mark out Korean food as different from the food of other countries in the region.

If you eat Korean food regularly you will come to know and love the sesame plant. It gives Koreans *chamgirum*, sesame seed oil and *kkaesogum*, sesame salt which is made from seeds which have been toasted and ground with a little added salt. Vegetables are often cooked with sesame seasoning.

Another national favorite is the soy plant which produces pods of beans which form the basis of *kanjang*, dark brown, deep flavored soy sauce. After the cooking of the soy sauce, *toenjang*, a bean paste is made from the remains of the fermented bean blocks and is used in many soups and stews.

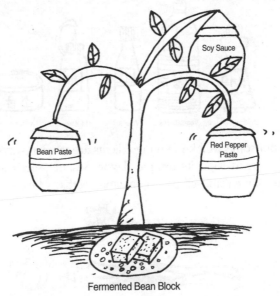

Fermented Bean Block

You will certainly recognize a third soy product, very hot to the palate, *kochujang*, a red pepper paste made from fermented bean paste powder, red pepper powder, salt and glutinous flour.

If you are in Korea in the autumn you cannot miss seeing an important seasoning in preparation. Red peppers lie in brilliant heaps on sidewalks and in courtyards, drying in the sun. When they are fully dried they are then reduced to powder which is obtainable in all grocery stores, coarsely and finely ground.

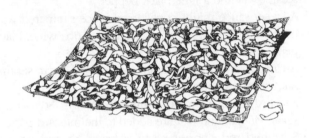

An unusual condiment is the green onion which is widely used during the cooking process to add flavor to a dish. As you become familiar with Korean food you will find that the onions contribute both a spicy hotness from the green leaves and a sweetness from the white parts. They should not be overcooked so they are generally added at the end of the cooking time.

Of course not every single condiment is hot. Like the rest of the world Koreans crave the occasional sweet touch. To give that touch to both broiled dishes such as *kalbi* or *bulgogi* and to dessert courses such as rice cakes, sugar is added. Cinnamon powder is also used in dessert dishes.

These are the basic ingredients used to give a tasty twist to Korean food. You will find that they are combined imaginatively in a variety of composite sauces used as marinades before cooking or as dipping sauces during the meal. Housewives pride themselves on the quality of their sauces. Traditional recipes handed down within the family are still acknowledged to be best. The test is in the taste.

- A seasoned soy sauce might contain soy sauce mixed with sugar, rice wine, green onion, garlic, sesame oil, sesame salt and a little black pepper.
- A sweet sauce might contain soy sauce simmered with corn syrup, sugar, water, sliced ginger, rice wine, black pepper and MSG to thicken.
- A vinegar-soy sauce combines soy sauce, sugar, sesame salt, vinegar, chopped green pepper and garlic.
- Mustard vinegar sauce is quite common. Soy sauce, sugar, vinegar and salt are added to the mustard paste.
- Seasoned red pepper paste is based on red pepper paste to which the cook adds soy sauce, chopped

garlic and onion, sugar, sesame salt and sesame oil. The ingredients are simmered together until thick.

The sauces are prepared and kept outside in a sunny courtyard or balcony to ferment and are at the center of the Korean cook's meal preparation. Modern supermarkets have ready-prepared convenience foods for the hard pressed housewife but you still see clusters of pots outside dwellings throughout the country. The tradition lives on.

A cuisine unveiled :

Korean dishes explained

The heart of a Korean meal is a dish of grains, often but not always rice, a bowl of soup and a couple of dishes of the national favorite pickled vegetable, *kimchi*. For a simple meal this alone would be enough. For a more complex meal, side dishes are added. They may contain meats or fish, vegetables or eggs and they may be cooked in a dozen or more different ways. At a Korean celebration the table is covered with dishes, some to be eaten by the individual diner but many to be shared by all, in a meal which is a veritable feast.

KUK, 국
A bowl of soup

You are sure to drink soup while you are in Korea. Koreans love a bowl of hot soup particularly during their icy winter. But year round it is served as the nucleus of a simple meal together with rice, *kimchi* and a couple of side dishes. You cannot miss soups on a menu. They can be identified by the suffix *tang*. Meats, fish and vegetables are used as the basic ingredients.

● SOLLONGTANG (설렁탕)
Bone and stew meat stock soup

This is a thick broth made from beef bones and stewing meat. Before serving the stewing meat is sliced and returned to the soup. Square cut radish *kimchi*, chopped scallion and hot pepper sauce finish the dish. The ingredients of *kalbi tang*, short ribs soup, are short ribs and stewing steak with radish and onions.

● KOMTANG (곰탕)
Stew meat and tripe soup

Two boilings are necessary for this soup. Brisket and beef entrails are boiled together and the soup and meats stored separately until required. Then the two are boiled together for a second time.

● UJOKTANG (우족탕)
Hock soup

It is beef hocks which are used in this soup. They are boiled until the glutinous meat is tender. The meat is then sliced and returned to the pot for eating. The meat around beef knuckle bones never gets really tender but they are the principal ingredient of *togani tang*, knuckle bone soup. The dish is prized because of its chewy texture but is, perhaps, an acquired taste.

● KKORI KOMTANG (꼬리 곰탕)
Oxtail soup

You will almost certainly come across this soup. It is very

nutritious and much prized among Koreans. The key to its flavor is long term boiling. It can be simmered for as much as six hours. The stock jells when cold but the soup is always served piping hot.

● YUKKAEJANG (육개장)
Hot spicy stew meat soup

This is a simple and popular clear soup made of meat stock to which a fiery sauce of red pepper powder sauted in fat is added. Be warned. It is not for a newcomer to the heat of Korean food.

● YANGJUPTANG (양즙탕)
Honeycomb tripe soup

In addition to the tripe, ground soy beans are added to this soup. Its milky color comes from its long cooking.

Another soup made from beef entrails is *naejang-tang*, beef chitterlings soup, which is served with sliced meat, chopped onions and radish.

● HAEJANG KUK (해장 국)
Sunrise soup

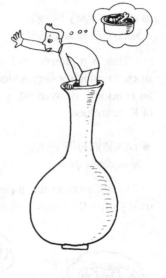

If you find yourself the worse for wear after a heavy night's drinking, this is what Koreans will prescribe for you. The soup is famed for its restorative properties which are reputed to clear even the sleepiest or most hung-over head. In addition to bones, chopped radish and radish leaves, cabbage and green onions, fresh blood from the slaughter house is added to give it extra body.

● CHUOTANG (추어탕)
Loach and bean paste soup

Bean Paste

This is a soup based on a fish stock which is obtained from boiling the loach. Soy bean paste and cabbage or turnip leaves are then added and the stock is simmered. The soup is served sprinkled with black pepper or prickly ash seed powder.

● MAEUNTANG (매운탕)
Fish stew

If you go to a restaurant which offers this dish as a specialty you may be required to select your catch of the day from an aquarium. The price will be calculated by the weight of the fish. The cleaned fish is cut into three or four pieces and boiled with ground beef and green vegetables such as watercress and garland chrysanthemum and the red pepper paste. The flavoring in this well-loved dish is fiery *kochujang*, red bean paste.

● TAKKOMTANG (닭곰탕)
Boiled chicken soup

A simpler chicken soup. The chief ingredient of this soup is a chicken which is boiled to create a stock and is then cut into six or eight pieces. The meat is seasoned with crushed garlic, scallions, sesame oil, salt and pepper and the boiling stock poured over the top. A tasty dish for the newcomer.

● TANGPA KUK (탕파 국)
Green onion soup

Tangpa kuk is an interesting combination of beef and vegetables but is classed as a vegetable soup in Korea. A robust stock made from small thin squares of beef, soy sauce, garlic, sesame salt and black pepper is the base of this soup which incorporates green onions cut into short lengths and dipped in egg.

An even more substantial variation on this soup is created when balls of seasoned minced beef and bean curd are added. Pine nuts hidden in the meat balls add a deluxe

SAMGYETANG, 삼계탕
Ginseng chicken soup

This is a wonderful Korean dish which is gradually being recognized by the rest of the world. Even if you are sceptical about the properties attributed to ginseng you will enjoy this dish which is said to give stamina in the steamy Korean summer. The body cavity of a small chicken is stuffed with glutinous rice, young ginseng shoots and jujube. The chicken is then boiled in a clear stock and served in an individual earthenware pot. Highly recommended for those new to Korean food.

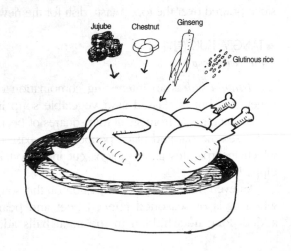

Jujube Chestnut Ginseng

Glutinous rice

quality of the final dish. Another soup with a hearty meat and vegetable stock finished with meatballs made from beef and bell flower roots is *Saengcho tang*.

● KONGNAMUL KUK (콩나물 국)
Bean sprout soup

Bean sprouts are widely used in Korean cooking and are a staple vegetable. They are simmered with garlic and scallions in salted water to produce this soup which, with a sprinkling of red pepper, is used as a remedy for the common cold. The sprouts have a crunchy texture.

● NAENG-I KUK (냉이 국)
Shepherd's purse soup

If you are served *Naeng-i guk* you are very fortunate. The wild vegetable is available only in the early spring. In this soup it is added to a bean paste flavored stock to make a stimulating appetizer.

● OI NAENGGUK (오이 냉국)
Chilled cucumber soup

If you visit Korea during the summer you will find it sticky and hot. The locals find summer weather difficult too so cold soups are popular in the summer in Korea. The base is often a mixture of soy sauce and vinegar. In this soup

Sesame

Soy Sauce ↓

↓

Vinegar

cucumbers and sesame seeds are added to this base. Steamed and seasoned eggplants are the vegetables added to *kaji naengguk*, chilled eggplant soup.

PAP, 밥

Rice

The Korean expression for "Have you had breakfast?" is "Have you eaten rice today?" This should come as no surprise as rice is one of the staple foods of Korea and appears at almost every meal occasion.

Two main varieties are grown. One is tap kik, the rice which grows in the lowland rice paddies everywhere. It is this which is used in Korean kitchens. The cooked grains are always short and slightly sticky when served. The other main variety is upland rice which is usually dried and goes into the milling of rice flour and the brewing of beer.

In the past rice was synonymous with wealth as it was a tangible way for farming people to calculate their worth.

● KONGNAMULBAP (콩나물밥)
Bean sprout rice

This is a simpler rice dish in which the important constituents are beef strips and bean sprouts. The bean sprouts are steamed gently above the cooking rice and beef mixture. Another dish combining rice and vegetables is *song-i posot pap*, pine mushroom rice. The added ingredient in this dish is chicken which is combined with the pine mushrooms.

● OGOKPAP (오곡밥)
Five grain dish

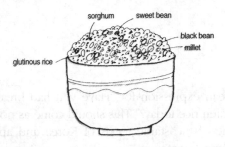

Rice may be the Korean staple but they also make use of other grains. Five grains are used together in this dish. Glutinous and regular rice, glutinous sorghum, glutinous millet, dried black beans and dried sweet beans are each prepared separately in the cleaning and soaking stages and then cooked until the grains have expanded and are well done. A very filling dish.

● SSAMBAP (쌈밥)
Rice in a roll

Koreans love to wrap their food up and have a variety of ways of doing this. When you eat broiled meat such as *pulgogi* you will roll it in lettuce leaves. At celebrations dishes such as the elaborate *kujolpan* use the wrap up method for intricately sliced vegetables and eggs.

But cooked rice is the most usual filling for a roll up dish. It can be simply rice, lettuce and a sauce but cooked meats and fish may be added to give a more substantial, filling meal. And lettuce leaves are the most popular form of wrap. As you walk around the streets you'll see that greengrocers often have boxes of loose lettuce leaves on sale for this purpose. Cabbage leaves, steamed zucchini leaves, sesame leaves are also close to the top of the list and almost any leaf big enough may be pressed into service. Seaweeds too are used.

● SANGCHU SSAM (상추 쌈)
Lettuce and rice with hot bean paste sauce

This is the simplest and most popular *ssam*. You make a parcel of rice seasoned with *kochujang* sauce and wrap it up in a lettuce leaf for a bite sized vegetarian snack or side dish.

You may be treated to a more elaborate *ssam* dish. Seasoned beef and tofu is mixed and cut into small squares

KIMBAP, 김밥

Rice wrapped in seaweed

Kimbap is Korea's most popular and nutritious convenience meal. You will find it everywhere everyday. At a picnic party. In schoolchildren's lunch boxes. And in the chilled compartment of every convenience store. *Kimbap* is a best seller.

The dish is made from *pab*, rice rolled inside *kim*, dried laver. It is an idea borrowed from the Japanese in the colonial period but Korean *kimbap* is subtly different from its Japanese prototype.

The steamed rice is not as heavily seasoned with vinegar and sugar as the Japanese rice. It may even be more Koreanized by the use of sesame seasoning. The fillings, too, are a little different from those in Japan. Much more meat is used in Korea — beef, ham and sausage, for example — as well as chopped eggs, parboiled spinach, lengths of cucumber and pickled radish.

The rice and fillings are spread on a slightly toasted sheet of paper-thin seaweed, rolled up with a bamboo mat and then cut into bite-sized mouthfuls with a sharp knife. The result is filling and easy to handle. Delicious.

PIBIMBAP, 비빔밥

Vegetables and beef on top of rice

If you eat nothing else in Korea you must try *pibimbap*. A very simple but popular dish *pibimbap* is a bowl of piping hot rice served in a stoneware bowl with a variety of vegetables, cooked and raw, arranged on top. The vegetables are to some extent seasonal but you'll find that *toraji*, bell flower roots, *kosari*, bracken, bean sprouts and spinach are frequently served.

They are panfried and then added. Your rice may contain ground beef and an egg may be served on the top. But, if you wish, both may be omitted making this the perfect vegetarian food. You simply add a dollop of *kochujang*, red pepper paste and some sesame oil and then stir the whole dish together for a risotto-like meal.

rice

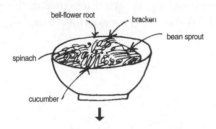

bell-flower root   bracken

bean sprout

spinach

cucumber

sesame seed oil

fried egg

red pepper paste

and white fish is steamed and then flaked. The lettuce, garland chrysanthemum leaves and thin green onions are set out separately on the table together with separate dishes of the beef-bean curd squares and the flaked fish. Then you put together your own choice of filling for the lettuce leaves.

● KIMCHI POKKUMBAP (김치 볶음밥)
Rice and fried kimchi

Every household has its leftovers. Korean housewives find that a useful way of consuming soured *kimchi* is to wash it and then fry it, adding any meats and vegetables to hand and some steamed rice. Everything is mixed together in the pan. Cheap and cheerful maybe but a wonderfully warming dish in the winter.

CHUK, 죽
Gruel

Do not be put off by the name. "Gruel" is not a promising term in English but it is an important dish in Korea. *Chuk* is made by steaming grain over a low heat until the mixture thickens into a soothing, unctuous liquid. It is good for the young and the weak and it is very often the first bowl you are offered in a Korean restaurant.

Simple white *chuk* is made from rice alone but the use of beans is also common. *Pidan chuk*, silky gruel, is particularly smooth as it is made from ground nuts which are added to ground rice before steaming.

● CHAT CHUK (잣 죽)
Pine nut gruel

You will be an honored guest if you are served *chat chuk*. This is a dish which was once served in the Choson court. Pine nuts still are scattered on Korean dishes to give them a touch of class. Pine nut gruel presages a lavish meal.

● PAT CHUK (팥 죽)
Red bean gruel

Pat Chuk is designed to warm the eater in the bitter days of winter. Red bean gruel is also

MANDU, 만두
Dumplings

If you have enjoyed Korea's noodles, then it is time to try its dumplings. *Mandu* are dumplings made from circles of wheat dough which are pulled up, like an apple turnover, around a stuffing of tofu, minced beef or pork, shredded *kimchi* and bean sprouts. Or they may be sealed around the filling along the side forming a crescent shape. They are simmered in beef stock and served with *kimchi* on the side. Traditionally the *mandu* paste was made at home but nowadays the paste is available ready cut in the freezer compartment of supermarkets.

MANDU KUK, 만두 국
Dumpling soup

The commonest way of serving *mandu* is in a meaty stock. It is very filling and warming in the cold Korean winter. A dish with small *mandu* like Western ravioli is called *pyonsu*.

said to ward off evil spirits and therefore bring good luck.

● CHONBOK CHUK (전복 죽)
Abalone gruel

If you have been sick you may be fed this highly nutritious dish which is often recommended for convalescents. In addition to the sliced abalone and rice, a beaten egg and soy and sesame seasoning may be added before serving. Seafood and rice are also the components of *yachae gul chuk*. Parboiled, seasonal vegetables and oysters are added to the rice gruel to form a rich, tasty dish.

● KKAE CHUK (깨 죽)
Sesame seed gruel

This is a dish which you will be able to identify by its color. It is dark gray. Not an exciting color, perhaps, but one which comes from the black sesame seeds which are soaked and cooked and mixed together with cooked rice just before serving to produce a gruel. A pine nut garnish is sometimes added. Water *kimchi* is the traditional accompaniment. Mung beans and rice are the base of *noktu chuk*, mung bean gruel.

KUKSU, 국수

Noodles

If you like noodles you'll soon feel at home in Korea. There are many noodle shops in town and country, selling products which are as good as any noodles in the world. In Korea noodles are made from either buckwheat or regular wheat flour. Perhaps the most prized are the thin brownish buckwheat noodles which are served in soups based on beef, poultry or anchovy stock.

● MAK KUKSU (막국수)
Handmade noodles

In this simplest of all Korean noodles dishes, you will eat wheat flour noodles cooked in beef or chicken stock and served with cabbage *kimchi*. But you may order a noodle dish which is a touch more elaborate. Small piles of thin noodles are served on a wicker tray, garnished with shredded crabmeat, egg yolk and egg white and cucumber in a dish called *chaeban somyon*. A seasoning sauce flavored with anchovies and kelp is served with this dish.

● KAL KUKSU (칼국수)
Chicken soup with noodles

Here is a dish which is hot and filling. Noodles made from buckwheat and potato flour are seasoned with *kochujang* paste. They are accompanied by a bowl of chicken broth and *kimchi*. Mung bean or potato pancakes often fill this dish out into a complete meal.

MULNAENGMYON, 물냉면
Cold noodles in soup

Koreans have found a noodle dish which is perfect for even the most sultry days of summer. Try it for yourself. *Mul naengmyon* is easy to digest and cooling on the palate. A dough made from buckwheat and potato flour is cut into slender noodles and boiled while very fresh. The strained noodles are added to a chilled broth made of beef stock and water *kimchi*. Your dish is presented to you, garnished with sliced beef, a boiled egg and slices of Asian pear.

There are some variations on *naengmyon*. In *pibim naengmyon*, the noodles are served with a hot sauce of red pepper paste, sesame oil and garlic and, on the side, water *kimchi* and hot beef consomme. In *hoe naengmyon* buckwheat noodles are covered with sliced raw fish and hot vinegar and pepper sauce. *Naeng kong kuksu* incorporates noodles in a soup base which is made from cooked and strained soy beans.

KUI, 구이
Grilled Foods

You will find that grilled foods are common on restaurant menus and are often cooked in Korean homes where there is little tradition of oven baking. Grilled dishes can be identified by the suffix *kui* at the end of the name.

"Koreans eat everything from the ox" is a Korean saying which you still hear. And it is certainly true today. Beef has always been expensive in Korea and so its use has been reserved for high days and holidays, occasions of celebration.

Traditionally grilled food was cooked over charcoal in a brazier. Some of these old braziers are to be found in antique shops today. The charcoals were put in a copper-lined well inside the wooden case. But today people use portable gas or electric rings at home and, in the main, restaurants specializing in grills have a gas burner set into the table, ready for use.

● TUNGSHIM KUI (등심 구이)
Grilled sirloin

If you are really sparing no expense, try a luxurious dish, *tungshim kui*. The meat in this dish is sirloin steak which is cut on request. After being seasoned with a mixture of sesame seeds, crushed garlic and salt, lubricated with some sesame oil the meat is cooked on a wire mesh grill over a gas or charcoal burner. Similar to *tungshim kui, anshim kui* is an expensive dish is made with beef tenderloin.

● TAK KUI (닭 구이)
Grilled chicken

Tak kui is a simple dish in which a chicken is chopped into medium sized portions before being marinated and grilled. You will probably notice that Koreans do not always cut their chickens up just as Westerners would. The cutting is rougher and breasts, thighs and so on are not necessarily separated. But the taste is just as good. *Tongdak kui* is a whole chicken, oven baked with vegetables and a soy basting sauce.

● SAENGSON KUI (생선 구이)
Grilled fish

Korea's abundant harvest of the sea gives you lots of opportunity to eat grilled fish. If you want to see all that is available, an early morning visit to Seoul's Noryangjin fish market is a must.

You will probably find eating fish simplest if you try it the Korean way, grilled whole with simple seasoning such as salt or soy or hot pepper sauce. Popular choices of fish for this style of cooking are *Yangnyom kui*, corvinas, snappers, herrings, *Sogumkui*, Spanish mackerel, sole and flounder. Grilled squid is called *Ojing-o kui*.

Shellfish, too, you will find plentiful and good. *Taehap kui*, grilled clams, for example, are opened and seasoned with sesame seeds and salt and served garnished with finely chopped scallions, sesame seeds and black pepper.

● TODOK KUI (더덕 구이)
Grilled todok root

This is one of the most unusual of the grilled dishes and the one you are least likely to find outside Korea. *Todok* is a mountain herb whose roots have restorative properties. It is available in Korean markets from March to May. The roots are peeled and pounded to tenderize them and, after seasoning with a red pepper sauce, sesame oil and sugar, grilled over a medium heat.

● CHANG-O KUI (장어 구이)
Broiled eel

During the steamy Korean summer, try a dish of broiled eel. It is a popular choice as its stamina-inducing properties are useful in avoiding heat exhaustion. You will also be able to test out the theories about its aphrodisiac properties. The eels are sliced longways and the bones removed before being seasoned with sesame oil, sesame seeds, soy sauce and sugar and then grilled.

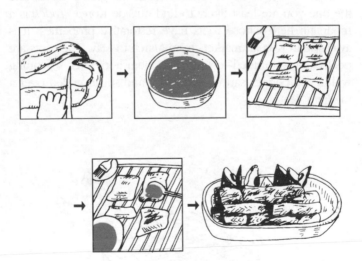

KALBI KUI, 갈비 구이
Broiled short ribs

You must try one of Korea's most famous grilled dishes. In a restaurant or at home, *kalbi kui* requires quite a bit of preparation but the end result is a finger licking, authentically Korean way of tackling beef ribs.

The beef short ribs are marinated overnight in a mixture of green onions, garlic, sugar, sesame oil and soy sauce. Rice wine and oriental pear can also be added for extra flavor. The marinade helps to tenderize the meat which is then grilled over charcoal or gas at the table.

You may come across a variation on this dish, *twaeji kalbi kui*, broiled pork spareribs, which are seasoned with sesame oil, soy sauce, garlic, sesame seeds and boiled ginger juice before being grilled.

PULGOGI, 불고기
Barbecued beef

One of the best known and best loved of Korea's native dishes is *pulgogi*. It is made from sirloin or other prime cuts such as top round which is chosen because it is marbled with a little fat but not too much. In restaurants you will find it sliced very finely, "paper thin." For an outside barbecue the meat might be cut a little thicker. Whatever the cut, the meat is marinated for at least four hours in a mixture of sesame oil, soy sauce, black pepper, garlic, sugar, onions, ginger and some wine.

You will find eating *pulgogi* a convivial experience. The marinated meat is cooked in a metal dish over the burner with whole cloves of garlic. Then you dig in with your chopsticks and select a piece of meat cooked to your satisfaction. Place this inside a lettuce leaf with other shredded salad vegetables and roll the whole thing up into a bite sized mouthful. Use the dipping sauces provided to complete the experience.

If your dish is called *Twaejipulgogi* you are eating barbecued pork. And with the addition of red pepper paste to the marinade the dish becomes the red hot *Twaejigogi kochujanggui*.

TWIGIM, 튀김
Deep fried food

If you like deep fried dishes in the rest of the world, you'll love them in Korea. They do not differ much from those you have met elsewhere but the range of meats, fish and vegetables cooked this way is impressive. They are not for the conscientious weight watcher but they are very toothsome.

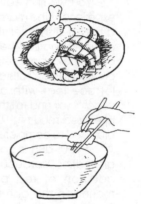

● SOGOGI TWIGIM (소고기 튀김)
Deep fried beef

Meat lends itself to deep frying. In this dish thin slices of beef are used and are served on a bed of deep fried Chinese noodles.

A more elaborate alternative to this simple dish is *sogogi samsaek unhaeng twigim*, deep fried beef and gingko nuts. The cutting and chopping of meat and vegetables is essential to the attractive appearance of this dish. Small squares of beef, carrots, onions, green peppers and gingko nuts are threaded

on to skewers and then deep fried.

● SOGOGI KKAENNIPMARI TWIGIM (소고기 깻잎말이 튀김)
Deep fried beef and sesame leaves

A mixture of minced beef and bean curd, to which chopped green onions and garlic are added, is the central ingredient of this dish. It forms the filling for sesame leaf rolls which are cooked by deep frying

● TAKTARI TWIGIM (닭다리 튀김)
Deep fried chicken legs

Chicken drumsticks dipped in egg and cornstarch are deep fried twice to create this dish.

● KUL & SAEU TWIGIM (굴과 새우 튀김)
Deep fried oysters & shrimp

Oysters and shrimp are plentiful in Korean waters and are often cooked in this way. You will be given a dish of soy sauce to dip the food in. The shellfish, is dipped in flour and then cooked in deep fat. Shallow fried oysters are called *kul chon.*

● YACHAE TWIGIM (야채 튀김)
Deep-fried vegetables

A mouth watering dish of infinite variation at a Korean dinner table, *yachae twigim* can be created from any seasonal vegetables so it varies according to the time of year. Vegetables which lend themselves particularly well to this style of cooking are lotus root, green peppers, sweet potato, onion, sesame leaves and chrysanthemum leaves.

The dish will come to your table with the vegetables all on the same platter which may be lined with an absorbent paper to catch the oil. Koreans often linger over this dish and are quite happy to eat it lukewarm.

TASHIMA TWIGIM, 다시마 튀김

Deep-fried kelp, Dishes for drinkers

Seaweed may not seem a promising ingredient for deep frying to you. But don't pass judgment until you've tried this dish of strips of deep fried kelp. An attractive way of serving them is to tie them in bows before they are fried. When they are cooked they are sprinkled with sugar and are a pleasant snack with drinks.

CHON, 전
From the frying pan

At almost any Korean gathering you will find pan fried foods. They are popular as side dishes at a full meal occasion or as snacks during the day or with drinks. They are served with various dipping sauces which give added flavor and cut the taste of the frying oil.

● PAJON (파전)
Green onion pancake

Wheat flour, rice flour and eggs create a pancake batter which is the foundation for a filling of green onions, watercress, clam meat and ground pork. These pancakes are served with a vinegar soy sauce.

● HOBAKCHON (호박전)
Fried zucchini

Many vegetables lend themselves to pan frying. Sometimes a whole platter of panfried foods, *modumchon*, is served.

Zucchini used to be known as *sungso*, the monk's vegetable, as it was so often eaten in remote monasteries. In this dish slices of the squat round, light green Seoul *aehobak* are spread with a filling of seasoned minced beef before being dipped in flour and egg and shallow fried. A similar method is used with peppers to produce a dish called *putkochuchon* and with mushrooms for *posotchon*.

Sometimes julienned zucchini are mixed into a flour batter and then fried. The dish is called *hobak miljok*. Grating the vegetable is the technique also employed in the preparation of *kamjachon*, potato pancakes. They are served warm, decorated with rings of red pepper and whole vegetable leaves.

●TURUPCHON (두릅전)
Panfried angelica shoots

For an unusual vegetable dish try a Korean springtime favorite known as *turup*. The shoots of the angelica plant are fried in an egg and flour batter.

●KIMCHI CHANGTTOK (김치 장떡)
Panfried kimchi pancake

The good Korean house wife is economical and wastes little. Even *kimchi* which is past its best may be soaked, washed, chopped and fried in a flour batter to make a tasty pancake. Red pepper paste may be added to give it a kick.

● NAEJANGJON (내장전)
Panfried veal kidney and liver

If you explore the Korean menu closely you will find that panfrying is a method of cooking not just vegetables. *Naejangchon* cooks slices of offal in an egg and flour batter to serve alongside other fried vegetables. Shellfish too can be prepared and cooked this way. *Kulchon* is the term you will find on menus for oysters fried in egg batter.

● SAENGSONJON (생선전)
Shallow fried fillet of fish

Any sort of white fish fillets — flounder, snapper, cod — can be used in this dish. This is a dish which goes equally well on working days and on holidays and celebrations. It can be prepared very simply. The fillets are dipped in flour and egg and then fried in a little oil.

But for a special party variation, *saengson yachae chon*, white fish is minced together with shrimps and then arranged with cooked strips of peppers, mushrooms and carrots in an attractive striped, rectangular pattern. The rectangles are dipped in egg and flour and shallow fried.

PINDAETTOK, 빈대떡
Mung bean pancake

A well loved Korean dish based on a pancake batter of ground mung beans and ground raw rice in the proportions of 8 to 2. The pancakes are fried on both sides with a variety of fillings. Ground pork, green onions, *kimchi* and bean sprouts are often used. Carrots, onions and ground beef are also popular.

POKKUM, 볶음

Stir-fry dishes

If you come across a dish with the suffix *pokkum* you can be sure it is stir-fried. It will probably be a combination of meats and vegetables and the juices may be thickened with cornstarch.

● MYOLCHI POKKUM (멸치 볶음)
Stir fried anchovies

You will need plenty of beer or water on hand if you order this as a side dish. Only small quantities are needed as it is very salty. The washed and drained anchovies are stir fried and garnished with sesame salt. Dried squid, *ojing-o*, is treated in the same way.

● SOGOGI PUTKOCHU POKKUM (소고기 풋고추 볶음)
Stir-fry beef with peppers

This is the most straightforward of the stir-fry dishes. Strips of beef are fried quickly with strips of red and green peppers and garlic. They are seasoned with rice wine and soy sauce, salt and sugar before the mixture is finished with cornstarch.

It can be made not only with beef but also with pork. The pork dish is *twaejigogi pokkum*. Add some *kimchi* and the dish becomes *twaejigogi kimchi pokkum*, stir-fry pork with *kimchi*. And for a really deluxe meal, you should go for *twaejigogi yachae pokkum*, stir-fry pork with vegetables. The peppers of the original dish are replaced by bamboo shoots, carrots, mushrooms, onion and cucumber. The final luxury touch comes with the addition of some quail's eggs.

● YONGGYE POKKUM (영계 볶음)
Spring chicken stew

Color is an added pleasure in this stir-fried chicken dish. Red and green peppers give life to the pale chicken pieces marinated with fermented shrimp. And no part of the chicken need go unused. In *tak naejang pokkum*, broiled chicken giblets, vegetables are cooked alongside the chicken's gizzard and livers. Other ingredients are mushrooms, green peppers, garlic, bamboo shoots and *konyak*, jellied potato cake.

● AEHOBAK POKKUM (애호박 볶음)
Stir fried squash

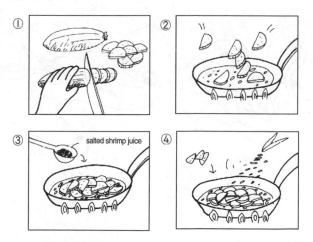

Vegetables are the cornerstone of stir-frying. And Korean zucchinis are particularly good. In this dish half moons of sliced zucchini are stir fried quickly after small slices of beef have been sauted. The two are combined and seasoned with sesame, soy, green onion, garlic and salted shrimp juice.

● NAKCHI POKKUM (낙지 볶음)
Stir fried octopus

Fish favorites which are cooked by stir-frying include sliced octopus pieces. They are sautéed with slices of green pepper, onion, carrot and garlic. Quick cooking over a high heat is the key to *putkochu myolchi pokkum*, which combines Korean long, green peppers and dried anchovies with seasoning.

● TTOK POKKUM (떡 볶음)
Stir-fry rice cake

Although it sounds unpromising, sliced rice cakes stir-fried with carrots, bamboo shoots, mushrooms and cucumbers combine to make a tasty popular meal. Try it.

SANJOK 산적

A meal on a stick

Sometimes Koreans want a variation on simple grilled beef and a more elegant, eye-catching way of presenting their grilled food. Like other people around the world they have discovered brochettes or skewers are good ways to hold meats and vegetables. The sticks of food can then be fried, grilled or baked.

● MANUL SANJOK (마늘 산적)
Sticks of garlic

An aromatic dish which features one of Korea's favorite foods, *manul sanjok*, is created by threading the skewers with cloves of garlic, cubes of ham and pieces of carrot and cucumber. The skewers are dipped in egg and shallow fried.

● O SANJOK (어 산적)
Fish kebabs

One of the features of Korean cooking is that cooks often serve fish and meat together in the same dish. Try *o sanjok*. It's a good example of this. Strips of fish and patties of seasoned minced beef are threaded alternately on to skewers before being fried.

●TONJOK (돈적)
Fried meat patties

This is another hamburger-style dish but fried this time. Patties of ground beef or pork and tofu seasoned with sesame oil and garlic and ground green onions are dipped in flour and egg and shallow fried.

SOGOGI SANJOK KUI, 소고기 산적 구이
Brochettes of beef and vegetables

These are quite complicated arrangements of sliced beef, mushrooms, onions, ginkgo nuts and carrots are brushed with a marinade of sugar, sesame oil, garlic and soy sauce. They are grilled, baked or fried.

You will find several variations of this skewered dish so examine it carefully to determine which of Korea's *sanjok* dishes you are eating. If you find rice cakes on your skewers the dish is called *ttok sanjok*. For *pa sanjok* your strips of beef are separated by the green tops of leeks and, for *twaejigogi kimchi sanjok*, pork is used and threaded alternately with *kimchi*.

An elaborate cold dish is made from pressed beef threaded alternately with cooked mushrooms, egg yolk and egg whites, carrots, cucumber and bellflower roots. It is called *hwasanjok*.

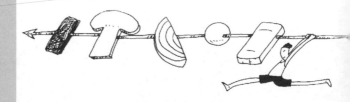

SOPSANJOK, 섭산적
Broiled beef patties

If you are looking for Korea's answer to hamburgers, *Sopsanjok* is one. The patties are made by combining minced beef with tofu and seasoning them with soy sauce, sugar, green onions, garlic, sesame seeds, sesame oil and black pepper. Chicken burgers are called *takkogi sopsanjok*. But they are eaten as they are, not inside a bun.

TCHIM, 찜

Casserole dishes

Many cuisines have casserole dishes, cooked slowly over a long period, so that much of the stock is absorbed by the other ingredients. Korean cooking is no exception. There are many casserole dishes containing different meats, fish or vegetables which are given the suffix *tchim*, meaning "cooked slowly." Steamed dishes, too, have the suffix *tchim*. Fish and shell fish is often cooked this way.

● SOGOGI YACHAE TCHIM (소고기 야채 찜)
Beef and vegetable stew

Here minced beef is combined with chopped vegetables such as carrots and green peppers and bean sprouts and balls of the mixture are wrapped in cabbage leaves and steamed.

● TAK TCHIM (닭 찜)
Spicy chicken

The sauce in this dish has an unusual ingredient, molasses or black treacle. The other essentials for this dish are chicken pieces, dried pollack, kelp and sliced red peppers.

● TOMI TCHIM (도미 찜)
Steamed red snapper

This is a family party dish in Korea and appears on menus in up-market restaurants. It is served at birthdays, weddings and holidays. The fish is sprinkled with white wine, then steamed and presented decorated with red pepper rings and nuts and mushrooms.

● MYONGNAN TCHIM (명란 찜)
Steamed pollack roe

Koreans are fond of fish roe. You might like to try one of their favorites, salted pollack roe. This is steamed and eaten by itself or is mixed with beaten eggs in a variation on a Western omelet. The garnish is green onions.

● TAEHA TCHIM (대하 찜)
Steamed stuffed shrimp

Another steamed dish but this time quite a complicated one. Large shrimp shells are refilled with chopped shrimp, onions, carrots and boiled eggs before being steamed.

Clams receive a similar treatment in *taehap tchim*, steamed stuffed clams. The clam meat is removed from the clam shells and is mixed with ground beef, bean curd, green onions, garlic, soy, vinegar and red and black pepper powder. The empty half shells are then refilled with this mixture and steamed.

KALBI TCHIM, 갈비 찜
Short rib stew

You will hear a lot about this dish in Korea. Koreans are proud of their method of cooking spareribs which are served at celebrations and which are often part of an up-market meal in a restaurant.

The ribs are cooked for about an hour with *pyogo* mushrooms, carrots, ginkgo nuts and jujubes in a complex sauce which contains soy sauce, green onions, garlic, sugar, pepper, sesame seeds and oil, pear juice, ginger juice and water. They are served with the vegetables and decorated with egg strips and pine nuts.

When pork ribs are used the dish is called *twaeji kalbi tchim.*

CHORIM, 조림
Seasoned with soy

Very soon you will become aware that there is a dish flavored with soy sauce at almost every meal occasion in Korea. And all sorts of ingredients are treated this way. The basic soy stock doesn't change much. It is made from soy sauce, sugar, garlic and ginger with some water.

In the past the rather salty sauce was a good medium for preserving food. The saltier the end product, the longer the food would last. Today it is just the national palate which demands lots of soy dishes on the table. Try some of them and you'll become a convert too.

● CHANG CHORIM (장조림)
Soy beef

A prime cut of beef is cut into several largish pieces before being simmered in the stock. The pieces are sliced up further after cooking so that they are manageable with chopsticks. This is a cold dish which can be made more luxurious for a party by the addition of red and green chili peppers and quails' eggs.

Rolls of beef stuffed with chopped vegetables and cooked in soy sauce are called *sogogi yachaemari chorim*.

● TWAEJIGOGI WANJA CHORIM (돼지고기 완자 조림)
Pork meatballs in soy sauce

You might be offered this dish as a quick lunch or as a starter. The meat balls are made of minced pork, ginger and onion, together with salt and cornstarch.

● TWAEJI KALBI KANJONG (돼지갈비 간종)
Spareribs in sweet and sour sauce

Pork meat again and the key to this dish is a good sweet and sour sauce. This is made from good quality soy sauce, dark corn syrup, sugar, ginger juice and rice wine and water, all slowly simmered together.

Another dish which calls for a sweet and sour sauce is *tak twigim chorim*, deep fried chicken in soy sauce. In it, steamed chicken is cut into pieces and deep fried before being simmered in the sauce with garlic, onions, green peppers and carrots. *Tak chorim* is a simpler version in which chicken pieces, carrots and gingko nuts are simmered together in the soy stock.

● SAENGSON CHORIM (생선 조림)
Soy fish

This method is good for the treatment of both large sea water fish and smaller fresh water fish. If you are presented with a large fish, it to feed all diners. Larger fish are simmered for a short time to cook just the flesh which you can pull off the bones with chopsticks. If your fish is smaller, it will have been boiled before being simmered in soy sauce so that its bones are softened. You eat it in its entirety.

Popular soy-sauce glazed fish dishes are *kodung-o chorim*, soy mackerel, and *kalchi chorim*, soy cutlass fish.

● CHONBOK CHORIM (전복 조림)
Soy abalone

Shellfish is tasty cooked in soy sauce and, for Koreans, there is nothing to beat abalone as the jewel of the mollusk family. It is believed to be at its richest and best in the spring and summer. Mussels cooked this way are called *honghap chorim*.

● TUBU CHORIM (두부 조림)
Soy tofu

You will come across tofu, bean curd, a lot in Korean cooking. It is highly nutritious as 90% of it is absorbed by the eater. Useful in soups and stews as it maintains its integrity very well, it takes on the flavors of the ingredients it is cooked with. Soy based stock is a perfect medium.

In this dish squares of tofu are fried before being cooked in the soy stock with green and red peppers and mushroom. The dish is finished when the tofu has absorbed all its cooking liquid. With the addition of pieces of beef, additional vegetables and *konyak*, jellied potato cake, the dish becomes *tubusogogi chorim*, salted bean curd and beef.

● KAMJA CHORIM (감자 조림)
Soy potatoes

Diced potatoes or sweet potatoes are the basis of this dish and may be mixed with green peppers or carrots or even minced meats. They are simmered in soy stock before being served.

You will find lots of other vegetables treated this way. Examples are lotus root which appears on menus as *yonkun chorim*; eggplant, *kaji chorim*; burdock root, *uong chorim*; and stuffed bamboo shoots which are called *chuksun chang chorim*. Salted black beans cooked in soy sauce are called *kong chorim*.

Cucumbers, uncooked but dressed in a soy sauce, are called *oi chang-atchi* and sesame leaves dressed similarly are called *kkaennip chang-atchi*.

YONGUN CHORIM, 연근 조림
Soy-glazed lotus root

Lotus roots, the rhizome of the lotus plant, have a crisp texture and a mild flavor and are things of unexpected beauty. Outwardly they are unexceptional, three inches across and two or three feet long divided into segments of about five inches. But opened up they reveal air passages which run the length of the rhizome and give cross sections a most attractive wagon wheel pattern. They are commonly cooked with soy sauce, deep fried or candied for special occasions.

CHONGOL, 전골
Hot pot cooking

If you go to a Korean restaurant meal and you find a burner set into the middle of the table, you may well be offered a *chongol* dish. It is another quick form of cooking at the table in a metal or stone dish.

You will see your food cooking in a swiftly boiling stock made from soy sauce, garlic, sugar, black pepper, sesame oil, sesame seeds and green onions. As you look on, you can give the dish an occasional stir.

Chongol dishes can be made of meat or fish but very often contain both which results in an exciting blend of flavors. Simpler dishes are part of the Korean everyday diet. The more complicated meals  are only prepared as part of a party table.

● TUBU CHONGOL (두부 전골)
Tofu hot pot

Tofu is a useful protein because it holds its shape so well during cooking, even in boiling stock. The tofu in this dish is cut into cubes, coated with flour and fried. Two cubes are then sandwiched together with seasoned ground beef and then cooked in the stock. Other ingredients may be mushrooms, bamboo shoots, watercress, bean sprouts and green onions.

● KOPCHANG CHONGOL (곱창 전골)
Tripe and vegetable hot pot

It is the Koreans' proud boast that they eat every part of the animal. Nothing goes to waste. The beef entrails, seasoned with red pepper, are put to use in this dish and are cooked with vegetables at the table. Cooked noodles are added at the end to fill out the meal. This dish is served as a main course or as a side dish for drinkers.

● TAKKOGI CHONGOL (닭고기 전골)
Chicken hot pot

This is a rich dish using sliced raw chicken meat. It is cooked with mushrooms, green onions, carrots, watercress, garland chrysanthemum, egg white and yolks, garlic and gingko nuts.

You will also find in it a noodle-like ingredient. You may be surprised to learn that it is made from potato. The unusual ingredient is *konyak*, jellied potato cake, which can be sliced and used like noodles.

● TOMI CHONGOL (도미 전골)
Red snapper hot pot

If you are served *tomi chongol* you are an honored guest. Fish is not particularly cheap in Korea and a whole red snapper is used in this dish. Slits are made in the side of the fish. They are filled with a mixture of ground beef, onion and red pepper. A variety of vegetables are cooked in a soy stock around the fish.

Rolls of cabbage leaves stuffed with spinach, bean curd, peppers, onions, mushrooms and clams are cooked around sliced octopus in *nakchi chongol*, octopus hot pot.

● KUNGJUNG CHONGOL (궁중 전골)
Meat, fish and shellfish hot pot

This dish is a good demonstration of Koreans' ability to cook meats and fish together in one dish. It is a combination of sliced beef, white fish, shellfish and vegetables. The stock may be beef or anchovy and noodles are added at the end.

SOGOGI CHONGOL, 소고기 전골

Beef and vegetables hot pot

Sliced beef, tofu and vegetables are the constituents of this dish but shrimps and clams can be added to make the dish even more flavorful. In the autumn try *song-i chongol*, beef and mushroom hot pot, as it uses delicious pine mushrooms which are available in Korea only between September and November. Another beef *chongol* is *obok chaengban*, boiled beef and noodles hot pot. The noodles are buckwheat and are cooked alongside sliced cooked meats, onions, watercress and garland chrysanthemum leaves.

TCHIGAE, 찌개

Simple stew

You may be a bit confused when you are starting out with Korean food because some dishes look very similar to the untutored eye. And there is only a fine line between a soup and a stew in Korean cooking. Soups are given the name *tang* and stews are called *tchigae* but a complicated *tang* may be very similar to a *tchigae*. A simple rule of thumb is that if you are served with a dish in one pot for all the guests then you have a *tchigae*. A *tang* will be served to you individually.

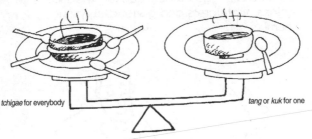

tchigae for everybody   *tang* or *kuk* for one

● TOENJANG TCHIGAE (된장 찌개)
Bean paste stew

If Koreans were asked to nominate a national dish, they would probably come up with this one. It is eaten very frequently in many homes across the nation. The key to the flavor of the dish lies in the quality of the bean paste and home made is best.

Bean paste is made early in the lunar year by soaking *meju* (bean paste blocks shaped like bricks) in brine for forty days and then draining off the soy sauce this produces and mashing the residue into a yellow paste.

The other ingredients of a *toenjang tchigae* can be tofu, clam meat, pork or beef but some stews are meatless. Any seasonal vegetable can be added such as zucchini, spinach, green peppers and onions, all seasoned with garlic, anchovies, red pepper powder and salt. A really rich *toenjang tchigae* containing beef patties, mushrooms, tofu and gingko nuts is known as *kungjung toenjang tchigae*, royal soybean paste soup. All these stews are eaten with bowl of rice.

● CHONGGUKCHANG TCHIGAE (청국장 찌개)
Fast fermented bean paste stew

Fast fermented bean paste is created by boiling the new

crop of soy beans in the autumn and leaving it in a warm place for a couple of days. Salt, garlic, ginger and crushed red pepper are added to the fermented beans and the mixture is rolled into small balls.

In the past the warm Korean *ondol* floors provided a perfect environment for the beans to ferment quickly. Today housewives increasingly buy the product in supermarkets and open markets.

Chonggukchang tchigae is created from this paste by adding it to minced beef, shredded cabbage *kimchi* or sliced radish, tofu, green onions or garlic.

● KE TCHIGAE (게 찌개)
Crab stew

Soft shelled crabs are the defining ingredient of this dish which uses also uses *toenjang* combined with vegetables such as radish and zucchini, garlic and red pepper powder.

● SOKKO TCHIGAE (섞어 찌개)
Assorted fish and shellfish stew

A cooked-before-your-eyes dish *sokko tchigae* combines assorted fish in a *kochujang* based soup.

● CHOTGUK TCHIGAE (젓국 찌개)
Stew seasoned with fermented shrimp sauce

Fermented shrimp sauce is a staple in the kitchen of every Korean housewife. An easy way for Korean cooks to give a tasty twist to a *tchigae* is by adding clear stock seasoned with the sauce. *Tubu chotguk tchigae*, tofu stew with fermented shrimp sauce, uses red pepper, garlic and green onions, together with sliced lean beef. The beef is seasoned with a little soy sauce, minced green onion, garlic, black pepper, sesame oil and sesame seeds. All the ingredients are simmered in rice water and cubes of tofu are added five minutes from the end.

You may find a stew where zucchini takes the place of tofu It is called *aehobak chotkuk tchigae*, fermented shrimp sauce stew with small, round zucchini.

Another quick and easy, everyday dish in Korean homes is *kimchi tchigae*. Sliced *kimchi* is sautéed and added with tofu and vegetables to some pork or beef in a hot pepper paste soup.

FROM THE FISH COUNTER

If fish is your dish of the day, you will have lots to choose from. It is an important food to Koreans because they are surrounded on three sides by the sea. Fish and fish products are to be found, cooked and raw, in many restaurants.

● Common varieties of fish found in Korea

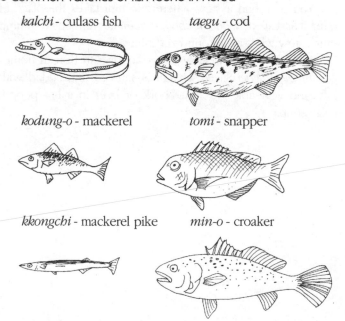

kalchi - cutlass fish

taegu - cod

kodung-o - mackerel

tomi - snapper

kkongchi - mackerel pike

min-o - croaker

pang-o - horse mackerel

paemjang-o - eel

nopchi - halibut

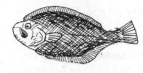

song-o - trout

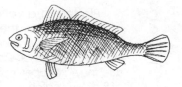

nong-o - sea bass

chang-o - eel

tyono - pacific salmon

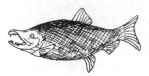

nakchi/muno - octopus

chogi - corbina

MODUM HOE, 모둠회
Assorted raw fish

Platters of a variety of raw fish are a common sight at the vast Noryangjin Fish Market in Southern Seoul and also on wet fish counters in suburban supermarkets. You can be sure they are super-fresh and include the best of the day's catch.

Sometimes you will be offered a serving of one special variety of fish. *Ojing-o hoe*, sliced raw cuttlefish is a much prized specialty of the ports on Korea's Eastern coast but is also available in other areas of the country. *Kwang-o hoe*, sliced raw halibut, is very popular with Koreans. They eat the flesh raw of this ocean-bottom fish also known as *nopchi*, and make the bones and trimmings into a tasty soup.

Skate or rays are caught in abundance in the waters to the south and west of the Korean peninsula. They are served raw and cooked. *hong-o hoe*, sliced raw skate, is soaked in rice wine before it is eaten. Fermentation takes place which makes the fish give off an ammonia smell. Koreans love it. Be warned. For foreigners it's an acquired taste.

Eels will often be seen in tanks at fish restaurants ready to be prepared to order. They are sliced and served on a bed of lettuce or sesame leaves in a dish called *kkomjang-o hoe*.

Raw oysters with *kimchi* are the filling for salted cabbage leaves in *kul possam* fresh oysters in cabbage roll, a dish which is like a quick *kimchi* sandwich.

All you need with these dishes is a sharp sauce. Korean vinegar-red pepper sauce or vinegar mustard soy sauce are just the thing.

● Shellfish

honghap - mussels   *saeu* - shrimps
ke - crab   *sora* - conches
kul - oysters   *chonbok* - abalone
taehap - clams

● Fish often used in dried form

tongtae/myongtae - pollack   *ojing-o* - squid
myolchi - anchovy   *ppyo-ojing-o* - cuttle fish

● OJING-O SUNDAE (오징어 순대)
Stuffed squid

A simple steamed dish is stuffed squid. The tubular body of the fish is filled with a mixture of bean curd, noodles, ginger, vegetables, nuts and the chopped tentacles of the fish which have been removed at the beginning of preparation. After the dish has been cooked in steam and finished by a quick boiling in fish stock, the tubes are sliced crosswise into attractive half inch rings which reveal the stuffing.

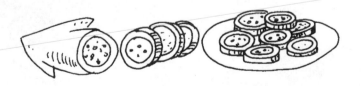

● CHOGAE CHOT (조개 젓)
Fermented clams

Salted dishes are popular as side dishes and snacks with Korean. They are also available in supermarkets and no longer have to be prepared at home. Their beauty is that they will last in a cool place for up to a year. To prepare *chogae chot*, fermented clams, the clams are mixed with salt and kept until the liquid turns milky which shows that fermentation has taken place. Then they can be used as required. You will be offered them mixed with vinegar, red pepper powder and chopped green onions. If you prefer fermented oysters, they are mixed with pieces of turnip, pears or chestnuts and flavored with red pepper powder and salt in a dish called *origul chot*.

● MYONGNAN CHOT (명란 젓)
Salted pollack roe

The fish roe used in this dish is salted and stored. Your hostess may have steamed it before serving or may serve it simply, uncooked.

● KEJANG (게장)
Seasoned crabs

A powerful crab dish made of pieces of seasoned blue crabs, *kejang* can be eaten raw or cooked in soy and water. It is seasoned with a fiery mixture of sesame, soy, garlic, red pepper powder and sugar.

● PUKOCHAE MUCHIM (북어채 무침)
Seasoned dried pollack

Dried fish is much used as a side dish at a Korean table. It is easy to prepare — a convenience food in effect — and always in the store cupboard. The dried pollack is shredded and seasoned with sesame, soy, green onions and sugar. Dried clams are treated in the same way as the pollack in a dish called *chogaetsal muchim*, seasoned dried clams.

MIYOK 미역

Seaweed

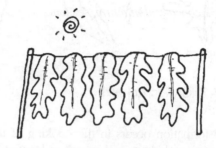

In a country surrounded on three sides by the sea, it is not surprising that every possible product of the ocean is used as a food stuff. Seaweed is a good example. It is a very nutritious food which is collected around the Korean coast throughout the year and is farmed commercially along the south and west coasts.

If you see bamboo or plastic screens in the water you are looking at a seaweed farm. The screens are seeded with seaweed and placed in the water. Seaweed leaves grow over the supports and are then harvested and dried. You may think that all seaweed tastes much the same but connoisseurs know better. They believe that the winter crop is the most tasty.

Three types of seaweed are widely used in cooking, *tashima*, kelp and *kim*, laver, and *miyok*, sea mustard.

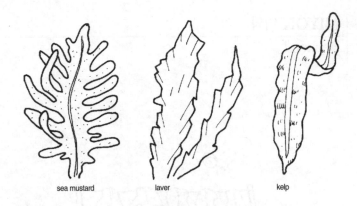

sea mustard   laver   kelp

● TASHIMA TUIGAK (다시마 튀각)
Fried Kelp

A transformation occurs in the cooking of this dish. The unruly fronds of kelp are cleaned and cut into bite-sized strips. When they are shallow fried they become green-gray in color. Then they are drained and sprinkled with salt and sugar. You will be presented with something which is a very acceptable side dish with rice and can be nibbled as a snack with drinks.

● KIM KUI (김 구이)
Oiled and toasted seaweed

You may think that oiling and toasting laver should be simple. But it is not as easy as it looks to get the fine seaweed sheet toasted evenly and without any black marks. *Kim* is inclined to burn easily.

But oiling and toasting is an art form that every Korean bride had to master in the past. For today's housewife, however, help is at hand as laver is readily available in

supermarkets all over Korea. It is a staple of the winter diet and of every child's lunch box. It comes in three densities each with its own special flavor.

● KIM PUGAK (김 부각)
Fried laver

Walk around a Korean supermarket and you will come across sheets of laver about five inches square being cut and sold. *Kim pugak* uses these sheets sandwiched together with a sticky, well-seasoned rice gruel. The bundle is folded and dried. When required the cook cuts the laver along the fold lines and quickly deep fries it. Sesame leaves are prepared in a similar way in a dish called *kkaennip pugak*.

All laver is not dried. If you want to try the fresh variety which has a flavor all of its own, order a fresh laver salad,

MIYOK CHABAN, 미역 자반
Sugared Seaweed

Potato chips are what come to mind when, in the chilled compartments of supermarkets, you see brown seaweed cut into bite-sized pieces, ready-to-eat and packed in plastic bags. The curly seaweed is shallow fried until crisp and then sprinkled with sugar and sesame seeds. It can be eaten on all those occasions when potato chips would be appropriate.

parae mutchim. It combines chopped fresh laver with slivers of radish or pear dressed with a sesame vinaigrette or soy dressing. *Miyok mutchim,* sea mustard salad is served cold with a sesame, soy and vinegar dressing or hot with a vinegar hot sauce.

● MIYOK NAENGGUK (미역 냉국)
Chilled seaweed soup

A Korean dish which is traditionally served to nursing mothers to restore them after childbirth *miyok naengguk* is made from sea mustard simmered with minced beef, sesame seeds, soy sauce and garlic. It is chilled and finished with the addition of cucumbers and vinegar.

NAMUL, 나물
Vegetable dishes

You will not have dined out in Korea many times before you realize that a Korean meal without two or three vegetable dishes is unimaginable. These vegetables may be collected from land and sea. They may be cooked by boiling or frying or may be served raw, salad-style, with a dressing. But they will always be present and they will always be well seasoned with condiments which are added by kneading with the heel of the hand so that they are mixed in thoroughly.

● SUKCHU NAMUL (숙주 나물)
Cooked bean sprouts

You can grow bean sprouts at home quite easily. All you need to do is to sow the seeds in a bowl or jar which is kept under a plastic cover to ensure that the conditions are warm and moist. But, like most people these days, you will probably buy bags of yellow soy bean sprouts or tubs of the more delicate mung bean sprouts at the vegetable counters of your local supermarket.

Washed and trimmed mung bean sprouts, *sukju namul*, are boiled before seasoning with salt, sesame, garlic and green onions. Soy bean sprouts, called *kong namul*, are handled in a similar way in this dish.

● KAJI NAMUL (가지 나물)
Steamed and seasoned eggplant

This dish uses the slender Oriental eggplants which are to be found in Korea. The vegetables are cut into half and then steamed until al dente, before being torn into strips and seasoned with soy, sesame, garlic, green onions and a dash of vinegar.

Eggplants cut into two inch lengths are used in *kaji son*, stuffed eggplant. Slits are made in the eggplant and a stuffing of chopped beef, carrot, cucumber, soaked *pyogo* mushrooms together with cooked egg whites and yolks, seasoned with soy, garlic and sesame, is inserted. Dipping sauces of vinegar-soy or mustard are served alongside this dish.

● OI POKKUM (오이 볶음)
Sautéed cucumber

Salted and drained cucumbers are mixed with seasoned minced beef and fried with soy sauce, sugar, green onions, ginger, garlic and red pepper powder. They can be eaten hot or cold, garnished with sesame seeds and red pepper threads. Sometimes dried zucchini is soaked and cut into strips before being fried with seasonings. This dish is called *hobak pokkum*.

● HOBAK NAMUL (호박 나물)
Panfried or braised zucchini

Zucchini is cut into sliced or half slices and cooked by frying or braising before being dressed with sauces flavored with soy, garlic and fermented shrimp.

● POSOT POKKUM (버섯 볶음)
Sautéed mushroom salad

You'll find a very wide range of mushrooms in markets and stores in both fresh and dried forms. Koreans savor them  in their great variety and use them in many dishes. For a simple mushroom dish, any type or mixture of mushrooms can be sautéed and used in this salad with other seasonal vegetables. The seasoning is soy and sesame and salt.

● MU SAENGCHAE (무 생채)
Radish salad

You cannot miss Korean white radish, *mu*. It is a common sight on the streets. Women sell it on the side walks and traders carry it about piled high on lorries. Perhaps it is best loved as *kimchi* especially in the spring when young radishes are very tasty.

But it is used fresh and dried in a variety of other dishes in Korean cooking. This is a quick and easy salad which often accompanies grilled foods. Match sticks of radish are seasoned with salt, vinegar, sesame, red pepper powder and sugar.

● TORAJI NAMUL (도라지 나물)
Bell flower salad

The root of *toraji*, Chinese balloon flower, is one of Korea's unusual vegetables. It is hand-torn into strips and dressed with salt, vinegar, red pepper and sesame for a red colored salad. To produce a white colored dish the roots are panfried without the red pepper powder.

KOREA'S MUSHROOMS

Common varieties of mushrooms available in Korea in fresh and dried forms

* *Pyogo*, Japanese shiitake, are grown on oak logs or on shii trees. They are brown and meaty and used in casserole dishes.
* *Sogi*, stone mushrooms, should be soaked before using.
* *Mogi*, Jew's ear mushrooms, are known in the West as Chinese Black Fungus and are gelatinous when cooked.
* *Kat posot*, parasol or umbrella mushrooms, are best when young.
* *Tulssari posot*, the field mushrooms, are often available together with their cultivated cousin, the button mushrooms.
* *Song-i*, pine mushrooms, grow on pine tree trunks and are used fresh or canned.
* Egg mushrooms, chanterelles, are long and pale.
* Winter mushrooms, Japanese enoki, have little flavor but are used for texture and decoration.

● OI MUCHIM (오이 무침)
Cucumber salad

Another simple salad you will find at many Korean tables is made from cucumber sliced diagonally into oval shapes and seasoned with salt, sesame, vinegar and red pepper powder.

● POMNAMUL (봄 나물)
Spring herbs

In the spring you will find activity everywhere in Korea. Even city dwellers put on their hiking gear and prepare for a trip into the countryside. Today they are going mainly for a day out. In the past they went to pick the first shoots of the spring herbs. The herbs were and still are a welcome addition to the monotony of the winter diet and they bring with them valuable nutrients which are absent in the cold days of winter.

● KOSARI NAMUL (고사리 나물)
Fern shoot salad

When you eat *kosari namul* you should always remember that this is a dish which originated in the kitchens of Buddhist monasteries. The monks lived on a strictly vegetarian diet, often in isolated locations. So they used anything that came to hand and fern shoots were plentiful and tasty. Gradually they were taken up by the wider population.

The new shoots of ferns are picked in the spring and are parboiled, dried and stored so this is a dish which you may be served year round. But the new season's crop, gathered in April and May and eaten fresh, is the most highly prized. It is served with a traditional dressing of minced beef, sesame, garlic, soy and scallion. *Chwi namul*, deep mountain vegetable salad, is prepared in the same way and is much savored by connoisseurs of Korea's mountain produce.

● NAENG-I NAMUL (냉이 나물)
Shepherd's purse salad

A dish of shepherd's purse salad is always the harbinger of spring on a Korean table. Technically a weed, it has a short season, March and April, and is increasingly sought after these days for its vegetable and medicinal properties. The young plant, a ground-hugging rosette of leaves, is harvested whole and the tap root below the leaves is cut off. The roots are then soaked, parboiled and then seasoned traditionally with soy, sesame, red pepper paste and garlic.

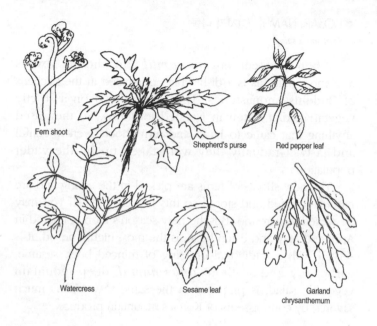

Fern shoot

Shepherd's purse

Red pepper leaf

Watercress

Sesame leaf

Garland chrysanthemum

● MINARI MUCHIM (미나리 무침)
Watercress salad

Koreans frequently complain when they travel overseas that foreign watercress is different from their local product. They are not wrong. Botanically Korean watercress belongs to the Evening Primrose family.

In this salad the aromatic vegetable is blanched and seasoned with soy, sesame, and vinegar. It may also be served in bunches alone or as a wrapping for pieces of squid or octopus when it is called *minari kanghoe*. Then it is served with a hot pepper-vinegar sauce. A similar dish is *pa kanghoe*, green onion bundles with vinegar hot sauce.

● KKAETNIP NAMUL (깻잎 나물)
Sesame leaf salad

Sesame is a bushy annual herb with green, close textured leaves with a serrated edge. In Korean cooking the leaves may be used as decoration and deep fried in a *twigim* dish. Young leaves can also be used parboiled, as in *minari mutchim*, or mixed with lettuce as a standard salad green. Parboiled and seasoned green pepper leaves, *kochunip namul*, are a popular salad vegetable.

● SSUKKAT MUCHIM (쑥갓 무침)
Garland chrysanthemum salad

Though they are native to the Mediterranean region, it is only in the East that garland chrysanthemum leaves have been grown for the table They are a good green salad vegetable in Korea. Mature leaves can be cooked quickly like spinach but for salads it is the young leaves which are used. They are blanched and then dressed with soy, sesame, green onion and garlic.

● TALLE CHANGGWA (달래 장과)
Wild garlic salad

Wild garlic in this dish is seasoned with soy and sesame and red pepper powder.

● SHILPA KANGHOE (실파 강회)
Green onion sundles

This is a complex composed salad made for special occasions. Strips of ham, cooked egg whites and egg yolks

KOREA'S ONIONS

* *Manul* - ripe garlic cloves with white or purplish papery skin. They are to be found in vegetable markets everywhere. They are also much used in Korean cooking, pickled and fresh, the peeled cloves sliced finely.
* *Tallae* - wild garlic.
* *Punmanul* - cultivated green garlic.
* *Chongpa* or *Tangpa* or *Umpa* - the common, medium-sized bunching onion, used in lots of dishes chiefly as a seasoning. It is harvested at several stages of development. Leafy stems almost all leaf with just the hint of a white base to the stem are about 12 inches long. Left in the ground a little longer, the leaves develop but can still be used as a vegetable while the white root base thickens into a small scallion.
* *Shilpa* - a sort of chives. They are much stronger in flavor than their Western opposite number.
* *Puchu* - a wild leek which is quite small and strong tasting.
* *Hopa* - cultivated leeks.
* *Yangpa* - dry Spanish onions.

are arranged in colorful strips each tied with a blanched green onion stem.

● MANULTCHONG TCHANG-ATCHI (마늘쫑 짱아치)
Garlic stalks in hot sauce

The above-ground growth of the garlic bulbs is much used in Korean cooking. The stalks are salted in bundles and then marinated in hot pepper sauce for a few weeks. They are served with a sesame dressing.

● INSAM CHOHOE (인삼 초회)
Ginseng salad

Young ginseng roots are shredded into thin strips to be used as a salad vegetable. Traditionally they are served with a vinegar hot sauce and a plate of lettuce. If the roots are steamed and seasoned with a traditional soy, sesame, sugar, garlic and green onion dressing the dish is called *misam muchim*.

● TODOK MUCHIM (더덕 무침)
Todok salad

Korea's special *todok* root is pounded, washed in salt water to tone down its taste and then mixed with watercress and dressed with a vinegar-red pepper paste. A different way of treating *todok* root is to mix it with well fermented red pepper paste and dress it with chopped green onion and sesame.

● KYOJACHAE (겨자채)
Salad with mustard dressing

A good mustard dressing is the key to many Korean salad dishes. Mustard seed is no longer ground at home but the

CHAPCHAE, 잡채
Mixed vegetable dish

If you are a beginner at Korean food, here is a dish which is very easy to enjoy. *Chapchae* is a well-loved Korean dish which incorporates virtually any selection of vegetables. Those in season have the best flavor.

The vegetables are fried separately in a very minimal amount of oil. Other ingredients are match stick-sliced beef and cellophane noodles. When each ingredient has been fried and the noodles cooked and cut into short lengths, all the ingredients are combined, sautéed quickly and seasoned with soy, sesame and sugar.

① ② cellophane noodle

③ ④ soy sauce

⑤ ⑥ soy sauce sugar black pepper sesame sesame seed oil

⑦ ⑧

mixing with other seasonings is still done in her own kitchen by the conscientious cook. The mustard paste must be mixed well ahead of use and kept warm for the flavor to develop. Then it can be used to dress sliced meats and fruits or jellyfish and cucumber.

Kyojachae is a dish from *Cholla-do* province which combines bean sprouts, bracken, radish, kelp, *pyogo* mushrooms and gingko nuts in a rich mustard dressing.

EGG DISHES

Eggs were once an expensive food so they were used sparingly in Korean cooking. Often they were saved for decorative purposes. They are still used today to make a dish look attractive. This is done by separating the egg white from the yolk. The whites and yolks are mixed separately, and fried into thin sheets of white and yellow "omelet." These are then cut into fine match sticks and are used as a decoration on top of food either mixed together or in separate color blocks of yellow and white. Cleverly Koreans have invented the rectangular frying pan so that there is no waste when the strips are being cut.

● TALGYAL CHANGJORIM (달걀 장조림)
Salted egg

You may come across a cold egg dish as part of the salad table. If the eggs have a mellow brown exterior concealing their white and yellow interior don't be alarmed. They are very tasty. Added flavor comes from simmering shelled hard-boiled eggs in a sweet and sour sauce of soy, ginger juice, sugar and water.

● ALTCHIM (알찜)
Steamed eggs

If you like a sweet egg custard then try Korea's savory version. A simple dish, *altchim* is made from eggs which have been beaten together with soy, sesame, green onion, salt and black and red pepper seasoning. They are poured into the cup in which they will be served and decorated with chopped green onion and red pepper. Then the dish is steamed for about ten minutes until the custard is firm but not overcooked.

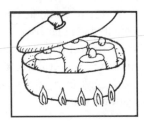

● PUCHIMGAE (부침개)
Vegetable omelet

Combining eggs with vegetables can be done in two ways in Korea. Omelets are popular and often filled with vegetables such as green onion, chives, zucchini and watercress. Sometimes eggs are cooked in a covered pan on a bed of fried mixed vegetables so they emerge poached, sunny side up. The dish is called *okchayuk*.

● TALGYAL OSAEKMARI (달걀 오색말이)
Five color egg rolls

The yellow exterior of this dish is made from cooked egg yolks. The yolk sheet is wrapped round a roll of laver stuffed with ingredients such as shredded egg white, shredded carrots, spinach, bean sprouts and mushrooms, giving the rolls an attractive five colored interior. The finished roll is sliced into bite sized lengths and served with a vinegar-soy sauce. A similar but simpler dish is *talgyal shigumtchimari*, egg and spinach rolls, in which cooked spinach is rolled inside an omelet.

TUBU, 두부
Bean curd

Koreans have developed many ways of eating bean curd which is an important source of protein for them. Here are some of the more common ones you will come across.

● TUBU SSAMTCHIM (두부 쌈찜)
Wrapped bean curd

The wrappings in this dish are blanched cabbage leaves which enclose a filling of bean curd, minced beef, shredded carrots, onions and green peppers. The bundles are steamed before serving.

● TUBU SOBAGI (두부 소박이)
Stuffed bean curd

Sometimes the roles are reversed and bean curd forms the exterior with vegetables within. This is easy because bean curd holds its shape well. Cubes of it are hollowed out and filled with a mixed vegetable stuffing for special occasions. For a luxurious touch pieces of hard boiled quail's egg may be placed in the center of the stuffing. The lid of tofu is replaced and the stuffed cubes steamed.

● TUBU SON (두부선)
Steamed bean curd

A simpler method of cooking bean curd is in a patty mixed with minced beef, garnished with fried mushrooms, egg whites and yolks and pine nuts. The dish is assembled and then steamed.

● TUBU NAENGCHAE (두부 냉채)
Cold cooked bean curd

Fried bean curd strips combine with strips of jellyfish in the center of a dish to form an attractive salad. Around the edges of the dish match sticks of ham, cucumber, carrot, egg and Korean pear are arranged in a colorful pinwheel. The sauce is garlic-vinegar.

MUK, 묵
Jellied food

Koreans are no different from other people in enjoying food with the consistency of jelly. What may surprise you is the way they make their jelly. It is not just gelatin which produces a jellied result.

● CHONGPO MUK (청포묵)
Mung bean jelly strips with vegetables

Mung beans are the first unlikely ingredient. In a time-consuming process, they are soaked, ground and strained. The liquid produced is boiled and stirred. When it cools it sets into firm jelly.

Blocks of mung bean jelly are available in stores today so one step in the making of this dish is made easier.

The cook slices the jelly into three or four inch lengths and adds it to match sticks of sautéed beef, blanched bean sprouts, sautéed watercress, toasted laver and cooked egg white and egg yolk. Everything is mixed together and seasoned with a soy and sesame and garlic dressing.

● TOTORI MUK (도토리묵)
Acorn jelly

In the autumn you will see people sifting through fallen leaves by the side of the road and setting off into the hillside with bags. It is acorn-gathering time.

The nuts are shelled and ground into a flour which is soaked and then boiled to form a firm jelly. The jelly is cut into strips the finger lengths and is served as a side dish dressed with sesame and soy flavoring and garnished with crumbled seaweed.

● CHOK PYON (족편)
Beef jelly

Chok pyon which uses animal parts produces a result akin to Western jellied dishes. The head and the hocks of the beef cattle are boiled for a long period to form a soft jelly. Before this cools hard boiled eggs, nuts and scraps of red peppers may be added. The jellied salad is served with a vinegar-soy sauce.

● HAEPARI NAENGCHAE (해파리 냉채)
Cold cooked jellyfish

Though it is not a manufactured jelly product, in the mouth jellyfish feels much the same. Koreans love this salad dish. Carrot, cucumber and cooked egg white and egg yolk are arranged with sliced jellyfish and are served with pungent garlic and mustard sauces.

A BANQUET
Special occasion foods

A Korean banquet will include many small dishes which you might find served individually at a more humble meal but there will also be some specialty dishes which require much more preparation and expense.

● CHEYUK POSSAM (제육 보쌈)
Steamed pork with kimchi rolls

In this dish pork which has been steamed in a ginger water is sliced and served warm with rolls of salted cabbage leaves packed with radish and other vegetables. A salted shrimp sauce is offered for dipping.

● YUK HOE (육회)
Korean steak tartare

This is a dish you will often find at gala buffets of which Koreans are very fond. It is not so different from the Western steak tartare. Chopped beef is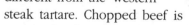
seasoned with sesame, sugar, garlic, salt and pine nuts and is presented on a bed of match stick strips of oriental pear. You mix the raw egg yolk which you find on top of the meat in

with the meat before eating. Offal is sometimes eaten raw in a dish called *kan chonyop* which uses sliced raw liver and tripe.

●SOGOGI SATAE PYONYUK (소고기 사태 편육)
Cold beef and salad

Pressed boiled brisket is sliced and served with hard boiled eggs, cucumbers and tomatoes. If pressed pork is used the dish is known as *twaejigogi pyonyuk*. Boiled brisket, *suyuk*, is a side dish offered in drinking establishments. The meat is sliced thinly and seasoned with sesame, soy, green onions and cucumber strips.

KUJOLPAN, 구절판
Nine Sectioned Dish

A special serving dish is required for this party dish. You can see it on sale often in lacquer ware shops. It is octagonal with eight compartments round the sides and a central round compartment in the center. Hence the name, nine sectioned dish.

In the central section, tiny wafer thin pancakes are placed and in the eight surrounding sections, vegetables, sliced match stick thin, are presented. Carrot, cucumber, mushrooms, watercress, egg white and egg yolk may be used and the skillful cook uses color variations to give the dish eye appeal. You select a pancake and fill it with the ingredients of your choice, roll it up and eat it with a dipping sauce.

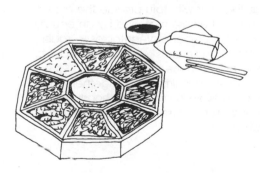

SHINSOLLO, 신선로
Fancy Hotpot

No party occasion in Korea is complete without *shinsollo*. Though it comes from the tradition of Korean court and yangban cuisine, the dish is made today by all Korean housewives. But only on high days and holidays as it is very time-consuming to prepare. It is cooked in a special *shinsollo* pot made of metal with a fluted neck in the center into which the cooking flame is placed.

The ingredients of a good party *shinsollo* are many. Beef liver and tripe, ground beef and beef brisket, fillet of fish, abalone and sea slugs, together with tofu provide the protein elements. They are matched by an equally impressive number of vegetables — radish, watercress and carrots — and nuts — walnuts, gingko nuts and pine nuts.

Everything is simmered together in the stock and everyone dips their chopsticks in to find succulent morsels when the dish is fully cooked.

OTHER KOREAN SPECIALTIES

● TWAEJI CHOK (돼지족)
  Boiled pig's feet

Specialist restaurants deal in this much savored specialty. The dipping sauce served with the sliced meat of boiled pig's feet is a vinegar hot sauce.

● SUNDAE (순대)
  Korean sausage

The sausages are made from the intestines of pigs which are filled with a mixture of rice, green onions, garlic, minced pork and noodles before being steamed.

KOREA'S BEANS

The ancestor of today's soy bean grew wild in East Asia and was cultivated by the Chinese as long as 4,000 years ago. The modern soy bean is extremely nutritious, containing high levels of protein, oil, calcium and vitamins and is much used in various forms. Fresh, as bean curd, but also as oil and sauce in Korean kitchens.

The seed pods are harvested from a dwarf plant and may yield one of three types of beans. Green beans are best used as vegetables and are comparable with a lima bean. They are very tender and have the best flavor. Black beans are used dried in dishes such as back beans in soy sauce. And yellow beans are generally used for tofu, soy flour, soy milk and soy sauce. The yellow beans are the ones which can be sprouted.

Sprouting beans can be bought in the vegetable section of most supermarkets in Korea. The most common are mung bean sprouts. But beans can be sprouted quite easily at home too using a plastic pot or a glass jar and keeping the seeds moist but not too wet. Mung bean sprouts also need a certain amount of pressure during the germinating period to encourage them to produce ethylene gas which causes them to grow plump and extra crunchy.

INSAM, 인삼

Ginseng

You have probably heard of ginseng. With *kimchi* and garlic it is one thing which is associated with Korea throughout the rest of the world. The name comes from two Chinese characters meaning "man" and "root" which refer to its curiously humanoid form which can be seen in the bottled product in many specialist shops throughout Korea.

The root belongs to a perennial herb which grows best in eastern Asia between 30 degrees North and 48 degrees North. Manchuria and Russia produce some ginseng but the best comes from Korea.

You will be able to identify a ginseng farm quite easily. Look for rows of plants shrouded in black polythene to shade them from the light. The Kyonggi-do area near Seoul is famous for its commercial farming of the roots which can be harvested from the age of four years onward. Real aficionados

think that six years is the optimum growth period.

You meet ginseng from time to time in the Korean diet. Ginseng chicken, for example, is popular and tasty. The root also has a long pedigree in the annals of herbal medicine. The Chinese first referred to ginseng as a tonic in the Chien Han era of 48-33 BC and subsequently they refer to it growing in Korea. Senility, diabetes and high blood pressure are all said to be helped by regular helpings of ginseng.

In Korea today *paeksam*, white ginseng which has been peeled and dried in the sun, is sold freely in the markets. A sweet product made from white ginseng, pricked and steeped in honey, is also available. *Hongsam*, red ginseng which is steamed and then dried in a heated room, is especially prized and sold under government control.

You will find very many processed ginseng products. It can be found made into an sort of instant tea which is sold in jars in every supermarket. It looks like pale instant coffee. Syrup and wine products are made from barley alcohol into which a piece of ginseng has been introduced. Cakes, candy, and jam are ways of consuming ginseng which would appeal to the sweet tooth. More directly it can be consumed as an extract or in tablet and capsules form.

TTOK, 떡
Rice cakes

You should count yourself lucky if you get a piece of fruit at the end of a run of the mill Korean meal. Quite often there is no sweetmeat. But times are changing. Ice cream, gateaux and fruits salads are now increasingly available.

No Korean celebration, however, is complete without traditional dessert foods, usually rice cakes and cookies. In this day and age the modern housewife does not have to produce her own. Today there are shops and department store counters specializing in these confections.

Rice cakes are sold in almost all big stores and even by vendors on the sidewalks. But buyer beware, they should all be eaten on the day they are made before they start to harden.

● SHIRU TTOK (시루떡)
Steamed rice cake

Steaming is a common method of making ricecakes. Glutinous rice or rice powder is mixed with water, sugar and salt and steamed with a topping of colored grains to give an attractive appearance.

A well loved example of this sort of cake is *shiru ttok*, which is made with alternating layers of rice powder and red bean powder in a 5-cm cake. *Shiru ttok* is a traditional offering at opening ceremonies when good auspices are sought. Even more delicious is *kongchalpyon* which combines glutinous rice powder, sweet beans and brown sugar in a steamed cake which is served warm.

●INJOLMI & CHOLPYON (인절미 & 절편)
Pounded rice cakes

Injolmi and *cholpyon* are made from steamed rice, pounded until it becomes smooth and sticky. The rice is removed from the mortar and, for *injolmi*, shaped into long rectangular bars which are then cut into pieces about an inch and a half long. The pieces are coated with bean powder to make them easier to handle. For *cholpyon*, the dough is stamped with a patterned press and cut into pieces.

●SONGPYON (송편)
Chusok half moon cakes

To make *songpyon*, the traditional half moon cake served to celebrate the autumn festival of Chusok, a more complex process of molding and steaming is required. The cakes are sophisticated products assembled with a great deal of painstaking care.

The dough is produced by grinding the rice finely and giving it color by the addition of pink food coloring to one third, and boiled mugwort to another third. The balance is left white. Dough pieces are  filled with a variety of stuffings such as jujubes and sesame seeds or crushed chestnuts.

They are steamed on a bed of pine needles to keep them from sticking together and to impart a pine flavor. After cooking they are washed to remove the pine needles and then arranged in a serving dish in an attractive pink, green and white pattern.

Other shapes produced this way are flat *tanja* and small balls, *kyongdan*. *Tanja* are small rectangular bars of rice dough, colored green with mugwort or red with jujube and rolled in sweet bean paste or sweet bean paste and chopped pine nuts. *Kyongdan* balls are given eye appeal by rolling them in chopped chestnuts or jujubes, cinnamon, black sesame seeds or soy flour. This gives them distinct color and textural differences. *Kyongdan* cakes are the Korean equivalent of birthday cakes for children.

Fried rice cakes made from glutinous rice decorated with ground nuts, jujubes and flower petals are *chuak, chon* and *pukkumi. Chuak*, walnut-sized dumplings are filled with a mixture of jujubes, honey and cinnamon and deep fried a few at a time. They are soaked in honey water before being served. The dough may be colored with food coloring to give an attractive effect.

HANGWA, 한과

Traditional sweets

● KANGJONG (강정)

Fried cookies such as *kangjong* and *yakkwa* have always been very popular. The most easily recognized *kangjong* dish is *kkaegangjong* in which white and black sesame seeds are prepared separately. They are fried until plump, mixed with sugar syrup and rolled out into golden and black sheets. A black sheet is laid on top of a golden sheet and the two are rolled up together before they cool. The resulting cylindrical block is then sliced into small circular cookies with a pin wheel design.

● YAKKWA (약과)

yakkwa

maejagwa

Yakkwa are honey cookies made with flour, sesame oil, honey, rice wine, cinnamon and ginger juice. They are pressed into a patterned mold and then deep fried. After cooking they are soaked in syrup and sprinkled with chopped pine nuts. *Maejagwa* are bow-shaped pastry twists, deep fried and soaked in syrup.

●TASHIK (다식)

The cookie cutter of Western kitchens is replaced by the cookie mold in Korea. Molds pass down through families and are chosen for the beauty of their design. *Tashik* cookies are made from ingredients such as rice, chestnuts, soybean powder, black sesame seeds and even pine tree pollen. The ingredients give bases of different colors which are mixed with honey or grain syrup. The paste is pressed into shapes using a traditional *tashik* mold which has several patterns incorporated in it.

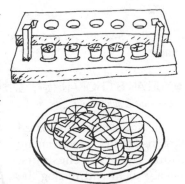

●KAKSAEKCHONGGWA (각색정과)
Candied fruits and vegetables

Candied fruits and vegetables, *kaksaekchonggwa*, have long been used to satisfy sweet tooths around the world. Carrots, pumpkins and sweet potatoes are pressed into service everywhere. In Korea less common ingredients such as lotus root and ginger roots, ginseng roots and even radish can be used. The vegetables are parboiled and then simmered in a sugar syrup until all the liquid has been absorbed and the vegetables are sticky. Candied gingko nuts, *unhaengkkochi*, which are cooked in sugar and sesame oil are another variation.

● YOT (엿)
Toffee

Toffee sweets, *yot are* made by adding nuts and beans to treacle.

● YULLAN & CHORAN (율란 & 초란)
Chestnut & jujube balls

In Korea other fruit-based desserts are made by steaming fruits such as chestnuts, sieving them and mixing the flour produced with cinnamon and honey and shaping it into balls. Jujubes are pitted and 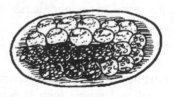 chopped and shaped in the same way. Both fruits are served coated with pine nuts and cinnamon. The chestnut balls are called *yullan* and the jujube balls *choran.*

Jujubes are also used stuffed, *taechucho*, with mashed chestnuts and simmered in honey and water until tender. They are served sprinkled with cinnamon and rolled in pine nuts. Dried persimmon stuffed with walnuts, *kotkamssam*, are also toothsome.

Fruit in season is also used to make jellies set with cornstarch and sugar. Cherries, strawberries and apricots may be used here.

YAKSHIK, 약식

If you are looking for a Korean version of Christmas pudding this may be it. A rich and well-loved dessert for a special occasion, *Yakshik*, sweet rice, is made from steaming glutinous rice and blending it with cooked chestnut flour, jujubes, raisins, pine nuts, dark brown sugar, sesame oil and soy sauce. The cooked dish is packed into small greased cups or molds and unmolded before serving. It should be solid enough to be sliced if necessary and is a sort of festive cake.

HANSHIK UMRYO, 한식 음료

Traditional punches

● SHIKYE (식혜)
Sweet rice drink

Tradition dictates that *shikye*, a slightly fermented rice punch should be drunk during the winter. But nowadays it can be found all the year round. The key to its flavor is a good quality barley malt which gives it a lot of its sweetness. The malt is soaked for several hours and then the clear water produced is mixed with hot steamed glutinous rice. The mixture is kept in an electric rice cooker with the warmer on for four or five hours until rice grains start to float to the top. Then the mixture is strained and boiled up with sugar and ginger. A final straining and chilling take place before the drink is served with some of the cooked rice grains and pine nuts floating in it.

● HWACHAE (화채)
Fruit punch

Most soft fresh fruit in season can be made into a refreshing fruit punch. Sliced fresh fruits such as strawberries, peaches, or watermelons are mixed with a little sugar for about half an hour and then added to a cooled sugar syrup. The mixture is chilled and served with a cinnamon and pine nut float.

With the addition of stuffed rice cakes, the punch becomes a luxurious *ttok hwachae*. A deluxe modern watermelon punch is made with a bottle of cider and half a cup of brandy added to the traditional ingredients.

● OMIJA HWACHAE (오미자 화채)
Omija punch

If you think you see tight little raspberries in the markets you have made a mistake. Many foreigners do. These are *omija* fruits. They have a similar color and shape to raspberries but are rather smaller and firmer. Their taste is very different. As its Korean name implies it incorporates five flavors — sweet, sour, bitter, salty, and spicy — which Chinese physicians believe have medicinal properties counteracting fevers and diarrhea. The punch is made by soaking the berries in water overnight and boiling the red water produced with equal quantities of boiled water before sweetening with honey or sugar. Pine nuts or sliced pears complete the confection.

SUJONGGWA, 수정과
Persimmon punch

If you have to choose just one of Korea's traditional drinks, let it be persimmon punch. It is made by simmering together ginger and cinnamon and sugar. The stock is strained and chilled and the persimmons which have been soaked are added before the mixture is left to stand overnight. The drink is served with a ladle so that each portion has a persimmon and some stock. A float of pine nuts decorates it all.

CHA & SUL, 차 & 술

Tea and Liquor

Do not leave Seoul without a trip to its central area known as Insa-dong which is famous for its tea houses tucked away in courtyards and old houses off the streets. The teas are based on Korean fruits and vegetables often boiled and dressed simply with honey or sugar syrup. The more popular teas are available in supermarkets in granular forms similar to instant coffee. They are acceptable to the busy though connoisseurs say that they are not in the same league as those which are traditionally prepared.

Examples of these teas are *insam cha*, ginseng tea, jujube *cha*, Chinese date tea, and *saenggang cha*, ginger tea. Less

well known are *yulmu cha*, Job's tear tea, made from a plant similar to Indian millet and *chik cha*, made from arrowroot, a very prolific plant throughout Korea.

● CHAKSOL CHA or SOLLOK CHA (작설차 or 설록차)
Korean green tea

Although it is not much drunk in the tea rooms catering for the tourist, you will still find green tea in a few places. It has a place at the traditional tea ceremonies at Buddhist temples and at special ceremonial occasions. The tea is grown in the south west of Korea.

● SSANGHWA CHA (쌍화차)
Medicinal tea

Not really the drink for a foreign guest or tourist, this bitter concoction of medicinal herbs, pine nuts, jujubes and egg yolks is designed as an all purpose pick-me-up for the ailing. Korea also has a tonic wine produced by soaking ginseng roots in alcoholic *soju*. It is called *insam ju*.

● SOJU (소주)
Korean liquor

The most common alcoholic liquor to be found in Korean restaurants, *soju* is a colorless liquor distilled from grains and sweet potatoes. It has a high alcohol content, sometimes as much as sixty percent and should be approached with care by the novice.

● MAKKOLLI (막걸리)
Farmers' rice wine

This milky colored rice wine is unfiltered so it is highly nutritious and still relatively cheap. It is not available in all restaurants as it can be kept for only three days at room temperature. Some restaurants have a contract with a supplier in the country who replenishes the supplies regularly. A good drink with pork and *kimchi* and, at 16% proof, relatively mild.

Other more refined wines developed from the *makkolli* brewing process are *yakju*, high quality rice wine, and *chongju*, refined rice wine. Both use better quality grains than in *makkolli* and the refining process is longer. In the end *chongju* is very similar to Japanese sake, as is *pobju*, pure rice wine from Kyongju.

● PODOJU (포도주)
Korean grape wines

Local grape wines are marketed under the labels Majuang, Chateau Montbleu and Noble Rose. Korean housewives occasionally make their own fruit wines by soaking fruits such as apples, plums or grapes with sugar in the local *soju* and keeping it until fermentation takes place.

● MAEKJU (맥주)
Korean beers

The local breweries who produce a variety of acceptable beers are Oriental Breweries (OB) and Crown.

Kimchi, 김치

Korea's own pickle

People who know almost nothing about Korean culture can usually summon up the name, *kimchi*, in association with the country. This side dish of fermented vegetables which is an essential part of any Korean meal is now famous worldwide and is actively promoted as a health food and delicacy in its own right.

The salting of vegetables to keep them through the winter when fresh food was limited is thought to have begun in China about 12BC. It was first mentioned by a Korean in the thirteenth century AD.

Early *kimchi* seems to have been a relatively mild dish, spiced with fermented anchovies, ginger, garlic and green onion. These ingredients are still used today but, after the

Japanese invasion at the end of the sixteenth century, the spice most closely associated with modern *kimchi*, red pepper powder, came to Korea. Cooks began to experiment, producing some throat blistering combinations.

Today Korea boasts more than two hundred types of *kimchi*, all rich in vitamins, minerals and proteins created by the lactic acid fermentation of cabbage and radish and whatever other vegetables and seafood are used.

The *kimchi* which is served at a meal will vary according to region and season and according to the other dishes on the menu. So a seaside region's *kimchi* will be saltier than that of a landlocked area and summer cooks produce cooling water *kimchis* to contrast with the heartier cabbage *kimchis* of the autumn and winter. And a delicate cucumber *kimchi* sits better beside a bland noodle dish than beside a robust beef stew.

If you want to understand *kimchi* at its simplest, think of it as divided into two kinds. Seasonal *kimchi*, made from vegetables that are fresh in the markets at any given time, is for short term storage. In the summer housewives may make a seasonal *kimchi* every day.

Kimjang (stored) *kimchi* is made in quantity between mid November and mid December every year. You cannot miss the year end flurry of *kimchi*-making. Even the most casual observer notices the piles of cabbage, red chilies and other greens by the roadside and on the back of wagons at this time of year. You will find, too, that clusters of black clay pots start to appear. Today they are not buried in the ground as they were in the past but are assembled on balconies and roofs, beside doors and in courtyards. In these *kimchi* is stored for a period to facilitate the fermentation process without which the product is not complete.

Modern life is changing Korean habits. You will find *kimchi*, ready-to-go, in chilled compartments in supermarkets, for example, so the working housewife does not have to do it all herself. But the tradition is still central to Korean cuisine. A family of four still eats about twenty heads of cabbage in the form of *kimchi* during the average winter.

● TONGBAECHU KIMCHI (통배추 김치)
Whole cabbage kimchi

This is the most common, classic *kimchi* you will find at a Korean meal. Whole heads of cabbage are trimmed to remove discolored outer leaves and then split longways into two or four sections. These sections are soaked in brine for three or four hours until they have softened.

While this is going on, the other ingredients are assembled and mixed together. These can be green onions cut in strips, match sticks of radish, chopped watercress and mustard leaves, chopped garlic and ginger, sponge seaweed and pickled baby shrimp and corbina and a good helping of red pepper paste. When they are mixed and the cabbage is ready, the stuffing is finished with a little salt, sugar and pickled fish juice and a helping of oysters is added.

Handfuls of the stuffing are then pushed between the leaves of the cabbage until it is all used. The outer leaves of the cabbage are wrapped round the whole to form a solid bundle which is then stored in a crock covered with salted leaves and pressed down firmly.

● KKAKTUGI (깍두기)
Chopped radish kimchi

Another popular *kimchi* which you will be able to identify very readily, this dish is made from cubes of Korean radish which are parboiled and then coated with a red pepper paste which sets them with a fiery deep red color. Green onions, garlic, ginger and pickled baby shrimp are other ingredients.

● YOLMU MUL KIMCHI (열무 물 김치)
Summer green water kimchi

If you have a meal during the steamy Korean summer, you will be grateful for this juicy *kimchi*. Young summer radishes and cabbage are key ingredients. They are blended with green onions, green and red chili peppers, garlic and ginger. A *kimchi* souse made of red pepper powder, flour and water is poured over the mixed vegetables before storing.

● NABAK KIMCHI (나박 김치)
Red water kimchi

The most highly prized of the water *kimchis*, this is an essential dish at a celebration. But it can be enjoyed all the year round. It has an elegant appearance created by the cutting of the radish into slender bite sized pieces of just over an inch square. The word *nabak* indicates the special cutting technique Korean cooks should use to create these squares. The word, by association, also has the connotation of something crunchy and crisp.

Other vegetables used in this dish are cabbage, green onions, watercress, red chili peppers, garlic and ginger. The completed mixture is finished by pouring a red pepper brine over it before storage.

● TONG CHIMI (동치미)
Winter white water kimchi

Small Korean pony tail radishes, soaked in brine, and green chili peppers, soaked for about two weeks until they have a slightly brownish appearance, are the major constituents of this *kimchi* which needs a fair amount of advance preparation.

Mustard leaves and green onions are also soaked with the radishes to soften them. Each of the soaked ingredients is folded up in separate small bundles. The final dish is assembled in its storage jar with layers of radish alternating with layers of greens and layers of chili peppers, thinly sliced garlic and ginger. The final *kimchi* is covered with brine and weighted and stored.

When you eat the *kimchi* you may find that the radishes have been sliced before serving.

● CHONGGAK KIMCHI (총각 김치)
Pony tail kimchi

This is another *kimchi* made from pony tail radishes and for lovers of fiery food. In addition to the traditional *kimchi* greens — mustard leaves, green onions — garlic and ginger and baby shrimp are added. Important

constituents, too, are fully fermented anchovies which have been cooked in a little water. The strained water is mixed with red pepper powder and rice flour to make a tongue tingling paste. This finishes a dish which is ready in a couple of days if left at room temperature.

● POSSAM KIMCHI (보쌈 김치)
Rolled kimchi

If you get a taste of this dish, you should count yourself very lucky. It requires a very wide variety of ingredients. Traditional *kimchi* greens and forest mushrooms are

spiced with salted fish and shellfish such as oysters and octopus. Fruits such as Korean pear and chestnuts are added. The whole mixture is garnished with pine nuts, chopped chestnuts, jujubes and red pepper threads and wrapped in softened outer cabbage leaves. Then it is covered in a pickled fish juice brine and stored. A luxurious festive dish.

● PAEK KIMCHI (백 김치)
White cabbage kimchi

Koreans are proud of the regional variety of their cooking. They will often tell you about a dish's antecedents. With this dish they have managed to keep some traditions alive despite the great political divide cross the peninsula for the last forty years.

Paek kimchi hails from the north of the Korean peninsula where less salt and red pepper are used in cooking. The cabbage is seasoned in an unusual way, using ginger and garlic strips and red pepper threads instead of red pepper powder. The stuffing, too, is especially rich. It combines radishes, mushrooms, Korean pears, chestnuts and dates with watercress greens and mustard leaves. A salted water brine tops the dish off before storage.

● MUL OIJI (물 오이지)
Pickled cucumbers in chilled water

Not all the *kimchis* you come across are complicated and expensive to make. Sometimes simplest is best. A cheap and cooling *kimchi* when short Korean cucumbers are in season in mid summer is *mul oiji*. The cucumbers are allowed to ferment for a week or two in salted water and pressed under a weight like a stone. You eat them with the chilled juice.

Pickled radish, *muuji*, often in long julienne lengths, is another simple, tasty pickled vegetable commonly served in

Korean restaurants. Also popular is pickled garlic, *manul chang-atchi*. Whole heads of garlic are cooked in a soy, vinegar and sugar sauce and then kept for at least three weeks before serving.

● OI SOBAEGI (오이 소백이)
Stuffed cucumber kimchi

This *kimchi* may appear difficult to make but a dexterous Korean cook can quickly prepare unpeeled cucumbers for stuffing. The skill lies in making slits in the vegetables but not cutting them through completely. The cucumbers are filled with a mixture of chopped leeks, green onions, garlic, ginger and pickled baby shrimp. The final dish is crunchy, juicy and refreshing.

● PUCHU KIMCHI (부추 김치)
Leek kimchi

Most Korean vegetables can be made into a seasonal *kimchi*, which housewives make almost every day in the hot weather. In this dish wild leeks, available in the summertime, are combined with pickled anchovy juice and red pepper powder and garlic and ginger. They are mixed well and allowed to stand.

● SUSAM NABAK KIMCHI (수삼 나박 김치)
Ginseng kimchi

Fresh young ginseng roots are cut into two inch lengths and combined with similar lengths of carrots, radishes and cucumbers. They are seasoned with a *kimchi* souse made from salt, sugar and vinegar and water.

KOREA'S MOST USED CABBAGE

Of all the vegetables used in Korean cooking cabbage vies with garlic for the title of the most common. Chinese cabbage, brassica rapa var pekinensis, is the variety most used in Korea as it forms the base of one of the most popular forms of *kimchi.*

This variety is the very hearty barrel type with almost yellow leaves. Prominent white veins fan out from a succulent midrib. The leaf may also be slightly wrinkled in appearance, earning the vegetable the soubriquet of "walnut" type. The base of the leaf midrib is slightly swollen and the leaves overlap to form a very solid base to the whole head. All the leaves are crunchy when fresh but the ones in the center are particularly crisp.

KOREA'S WELL LOVED RADISH

In the Orient *mu*, the radish is a very important vegetable, widely grown and widely used. In Korea it is used raw in salads, cooked as a vegetable and pickled in *kimchi.* A typical radish is between 4 inches and 24 inches long, tapered and spindle shaped with a slight point at the end but smaller spindle shaped ones and smaller spherical ones are grown in clay soils.

KOREAN CHOPPING SLICING TECHNIQUES

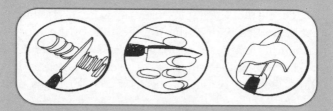

Many Korean recipes are labor intensive. Chopping and slicing are crucial skills for the Korean cook. Vegetables particularly have to be cut, not in a haphazard fashion but in a very special way, with very precise results.

A competent Korean cook has to master the sixteen different cutting procedures. The three most basic ones are the straight cut, the diagonal cut and the turning cut.

The straight cut would be employed slicing cucumbers, for example. The cucumbers would be cut into two inch lengths and then sliced lengthways into rectangles. Simply  cutting them across into circular slices is rarely seen in Korea.

 The diagonal cut is frequently used on meat which is sliced diagonally with the blade of the knife at an angle of 45 degrees. Chefs around the world acknowledge this as the best way to ensure tender meat as it cuts across the meat fibers. Round vegetables are sometimes cut this way to give an oval effect.

The turning cut is much used in making pickles and for chopping large vegetables such as radish. It is basically a straight cut but the vegetable is turned as the cutting progresses. A carrot, for example, is cut a few times lengthwise and then rolled over to rest on its flat side for a few more lengthwise cuts and then rolled again. This method keeps the vegetable from slipping and always exposes the largest area for the cook to grasp.

Dealing effectively with the knife is important. Korean cooks hold the knife in their right hand and grasp the vegetable with the left, four fingers on top and the thumb underneath. They push the food towards the knife and, keeping the tip of the knife on the chopping surface, raise the handle and bring it down on the food to be sliced. Essentially the knife is kept stationary. It is the food which moves.

Other salted and fermented dishes

Fish is particularly good for salting and fermenting. The finished dishes are stored and used in further *kimchi* making or served as a side dish or as a snack with drinks.

● ORIGUL CHOT (어리굴젓)
Salted and spiced oysters

Oysters are salted for three days and then seasoned with red pepper powder, sugar, garlic and ginger. They are stored in a jar in a cool place until required.

● MYONGNAN CHOT (명란젓)
Salted pollack roe

The pollack roe is salted overnight and then placed in a jar, layered alternately with a mixture of red pepper powder, salt, garlic and green ginger. The jar is closely sealed and left for three weeks. The roes are sprinkled with sesame oil and sesame seed before serving.

● CHANGNAN CHOT (창란젓)
Salted pollack guts

This is a good example of Koreans wasting nothing, not even fish guts. Pollack entrails are cleaned and pressed in a cloth under a heavy weight overnight before being salted for another twenty four hours. The salted guts mixed with garlic, ginger and red pepper powder are put in a jar and allowed to stand for about two weeks. The dish is finished by the addition of salted radish and more garlic and red pepper powder. It needs to stand for three or four days before serving.

Another dish which requires a couple of weeks to ripen is *kajami shikae*, salted sole, which is mixed with garlic, red pepper powder and cooked boiled millet before storing. It is finished with the addition of salted radish strips, more garlic, ginger and red pepper powder. The mixture is sealed in a jar until required.

● KE CHOT (게젓)
Salted crab

Shelled crabs are salted and cut into pieces. The seasoning used is soy sauce, garlic, sesame seeds, ginger, sugar, sesame oil and red pepper threads together  with MSG. It must be added at least two hours before serving. The crab meat can be returned to its shell for serving. These crabs must be eaten within a couple of days. For longer storage, the soy seasoning is boiled and poured over the crabs after it has cooled. *Kkolttugijot*, pickled squid, is prepared in the same way but the seasoning contains a very high proportion of red pepper powder rather than soy sauce.

The Big Occasion:
Cooking for Special Days

● HANJONGSHIK (한정식)
Korean table d'hote

Hanjongshik, table d'hote menus, are served at many restaurants in Korea. Customarily dishes are arranged on a low table. This is then carried in and set before the diners. Many celebratory occasions are designated as "tables."

Every Korean meal has rice, soup and *kimchi* as its center. Then it may have three, five, seven or even nine extra dishes or *chops*, as they are known. They will include a variety of fresh and dried fish, meats, fruits and vegetables. The complexity and the hospitality of the meal is judged by the number of *chops* served. At its most lavish a hanjongshik meal is a banquet. Seven or nine *chops* would constitute a real celebration and would undoubtedly include party dishes such as *shinsollo* or *kujolpan*.

What you see is what you get. The arrangement is such that all diners can reach all dishes easily. In general rice and soup are immediately in front of the diner in the first row. In the second row are sauces. The third row is made up with the cold dishes on the left and the warm dishes with broth on the right. The fourth row is arranged with vegetables on the left, *kimchis* in the middle and warm dishes without broth on the right.

You select at will from the dishes and put your choice on your own plate. You may drink barley water, *bori cha,* or beer with the meal. After the meal, fruit and tea or punch may arrive as a dessert.

● PANSANG (반상)
A minor feast

You may receive an invitation to a hearty dinner called a *pansang*. This is less of a celebration but still a stomach swelling occasion. A seven *chop* pansang might contain boiled rice, soup, soy sauce, vinegar-red pepper paste, two kinds of *kimchi*, fish soup, rib stew, broiled beef patties, skewered beef and mushrooms, a shellfish dish, mung bean pancakes, salted cucumber in vinegar sauce and broiled fillet of fish.

● CHUANSANG (주안상)
A drinking table

If your hosts offer to take you out for a drink, be prepared for some serious eating too. On a drinking table there are even more dishes than for a *pansang* and the balance of the meal is towards fish and vegetables rather than

meat. Salty food encourages drinking.

The menu might include skewered gingko nuts, walnuts, pine nuts, stuffed jujubes, *tashima twigim* or deep fried kelp bows, dried pollack, sliced boiled beef, steamed shrimp, *pindaettok* or mung bean pancakes, *sanjok* or skewered foods and vegetable salad. Again you will have your own plate and dishes of sauces and then you select what you want from what is offered.

There is often music and entertainment at a *chuansang*. When a dish of hot noodles arrives, you should start to make your farewells. Noodles are a symbolic way of saying goodbye and wishing you a long life.

● TOLSANG (돌상)
First Birthday

A baby's first birthday is an occasion to invite friends and

family. Delicacies will be laid out for the adult guests but there will also be a special small table for the baby himself.

The table is covered with many objects put there for their symbolic significance. All one year olds are offered noodles, stuffed jujubes, several different types of rice cakes, fruits, millet dumplings and rice, white cotton and banknotes. If the child is a boy, bows and arrows, a calligraphy brush, a scroll and a book of Chinese characters will be there. If the child is a girl, colored thread, a measuring tape, an iron and a book in Korean are added.

Everyone watches with interest to see which things the child seizes first as the choice is thought to indicate his fortune. Noodles and white thread promise a long life. Rice and banknotes presage wealth.

● PYEBAEKSANG (폐백상)
Wedding Day

Immediately after the wedding ceremony the new bride pays her respects to her in-laws in a pyebaek ceremony. As well as making her first deep bow to them, she offers them gifts on a pyebaek table.

The food is very formal, consisting of wine and chicken or beef jerky, stuffed jujubes, broiled beef patties, chestnuts and a nine sectioned dish of delicacies such as nuts and dried foods.

The in-laws throw some of the jujubes into the bride's skirt indicating their wish for her to have many sons. The bride is expected to eat the jujubes for good luck.

● MANGSANG (망상)
Sixtieth Birthday

Koreans believe that a sixtieth birthday is one of life's special milestones as five revolutions of the Chinese zodiac have been completed. The children of the celebrant throw the party and the table is called a mangsang. Sometimes as many as fifteen delicacies are served.

● SOLSANG (설상)
New Year's Day

New Year's Day is much celebrated in Korea as a time for honoring one's ancestors and for making a fresh start in one's own life with the start of a new year. The food takes many days of preparation and the main meal is always a full banquet. Traditionally the soup drunk on New Year's Day is rice cake soup. In addition to that, all the best Korean party dishes and family favorites are served.

● CHUSOK (추석)
Autumn Harvest Festival

This is one of the biggest festivals of the Korean year and marks the bringing in of the abundance of the harvest before the onslaught of winter. New clothes are worn and the best of the season's crop of fruits such as persimmons, chestnuts,

apples and pears, cereals and wine are placed on ceremonial tables to honor the ancestors.

Much anticipated Chusok foods include *songpyon,* the stuffed half moon shaped rice cakes and a beef and *song-i* mushroom soup. After that well-loved family delicacies and cooks' specialties are served in a grand, celebratory family meal.

Province by Province:
Regional Cooking in Korea

Korea is a small country but one with strongly held regional pride. One way in which local diversity is manifested is in its cooking. Rice and *kimchi* are common to the diet of the whole country but, after that, there are many differences in recipes and styles of cooking.

Seoul, the South Korean capital, Kaesong in North Korea, which was the capital of the country under the Koryo Dynasty, and Chonju in the south of the peninsula are generally rated to be culinary leaders.

Rural areas have specialties derived from the crops they farm. Some of these have been adopted all over the country as social mobility, increased prosperity and better communications combine to produce a more homogeneous national culinary culture. But many menus still acknowledge the regional antecedents of their dishes in names such as "Pyongyang-style" or "Chonju-style."

① Seoul Area

As befits the capital city of a nation and an urban conurbation of more than 11 million people, there is an air of sophistication about Seoul which shows itself in its cooking. "Nothing to excess" might be its motto as both salt and pepper spices are used with care. And eye appeal has its place so the size of portions and the arrangement of the food is important.

Dumplings, for example, are smaller and more elegant in the capital. Other dishes associated with Seoul are *sollongtang*, beef bone and tripe soup; *kujolpan*, nine section dish; *chat chuk*, pine nut gruel; *yukpo*, beef jerky; *yakshik*, glutinous rice cakes.

② Kyonggi-do Area

This area of Korea between the Western Sea and the mountains is very fertile and so has a wide variety of agricultural products to draw on. Cereal crops give the cooks the ingredients for good dishes of glutinous rice. The rice is sometimes cooked alone and sometimes with other grains.

Sujebi, dumplings made of flour and cooked with zucchini, red beans and maize, is another staple. *Pyonsu*, dumplings; *choraeng-i ttokkuk*, rice cake soup; *samgyetang*, ginseng chicken soup; *mu pinul kimchi*, stuffed radish *kimchi*; and *yakkwa*, fried rice cake are typical dishes from this area.

③ Chungchong-do Area

This is an area sometimes mocked for its rustic simplicity. Whatever the truth of these quips, its cooking certainly shows an unsophisticated charm using basic ingredients, sparingly seasoned and with an emphasis on economy.

Barley is widely used and *toenjang tchigae*, bean paste stew, appears frequently on the table. Other dishes include grains cooked together such as rice with bean sprouts; *shiregi kuk*, a soup using the outer leaves of cabbage; *oiji*, pickled cucumbers; *origul chot*, fermented oysters; and *hobak kkulttanji*, pumpkin cooked with honey.

④ Kangwon-do Area

Kangwon-do is on the eastern side of the peninsula and embraces a mountainous area and a long sea coast. The high land part is famous for producing potatoes, corn, buckwheat, acorns and many wild mountain vegetables all of which are used in its cooking to the exclusion of meat and fish. The region's other abundance, seafood, is used by Kangwon-do cooks on the coast where seafood restaurants abound.

Typical dishes are *kamja chon*, potato based dumplings and pancakes, and potatoes cooked with rice together with mountain herbs; *totori muk*, acorn jelly, and mushrooms. Various fresh seaweeds, pollack soup and squid *pulgogi* are also served. Desserts derived from potatoes and corn flours are made and *omija* punch and *tanggui* and corn teas finish the meal.

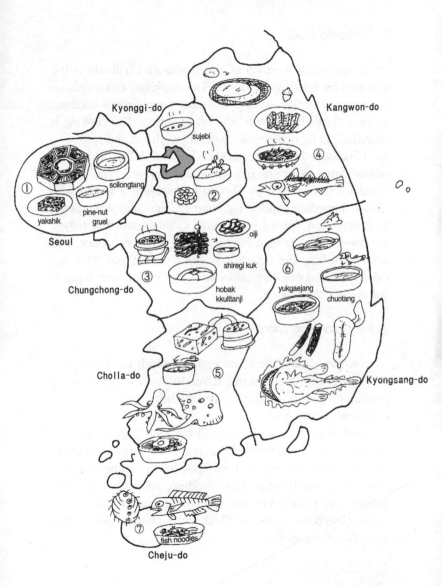

Kyonggi-do

Kangwon-do

sujebi

①

sollongtang

②

④

yakshik   pine-nut
             gruel

Seoul

oiji

③

shiregi kuk

⑥

Chungchong-do

hobak
kkulttanji

yukgaejang   chuotang

Cholla-do

⑤

Kyongsang-do

⑦

fish noodles

Cheju-do

⑤ Cholla-do Area

At the south west tip of the peninsula Cholla-do is the best area for gourmands to visit. The wealth of its agriculture, its proximity to the sea and its balmy temperatures combine to make meals here lavish and full of variety. The cooking is characterized by perceptible seasoning with salt and spices.

Chotkal, fermented seafood dishes and dishes using *kong namul*, large bean sprouts, are much enjoyed. The area is noted for dishes such as *Chonju pibimpap*, rice mixed with various ingredients including bean sprouts, and *kongnamul kukpap*, bean sprout soup with rice; *kkomak muchim*, seasoned clams, *hong-o hoe*, seasoned raw thornaback, and *sannakchi hoe*, live octopus; *hobak siru ttok*, pumpkin rice cakes, *kam injolmi*, rice cakes with persimmon and *koguma yot*, sweet potato toffee.

⑥ Kyongsang-do Area

"Simple," "salty," "hot" are epithets which can be applied to Kyongsang-do cooking from Korea's south eastern province. Fish is readily available here and used more commonly than meat.

Dishes to look out for are *Chinju pibimpap*, mixed rice; *tak kal kuksu*, homemade chicken noodle soup; *agu tchim*, very hot simmered fish, and *midodok tchim*, simmered clams; *chuo tang*, loach soup, *ttaro kukpap*, soup and rice, and *yukgaejang*, spicy beef soup; *tashima chonggwa*, sweet kelp, *uong chonggwa*, sweet burdock, and *chapgok misutgaru*, grain flavored punch.

⑦ Cheju-do Island

Due to its isolation until relatively recently, Cheju-do cuisine has retained a very distinctive character. It is simple with few dishes. It uses many of the island's famous products such as abalone and pheasants. Because of the island's mild climate *kimjang*, winter *kimchi*, is less important than in other areas of the country.

Special Cheju dishes are *chonbok chuk*, abalone rice gruel; *haemul kuksu*, fish noodles; bracken soup; *okdomi kui*, broiled tile fish, and broiled pheasant meat; *omegi ttok* and *bing ttok*, rice cakes, and *pori yot* and *kuwang yot*, toffee. Tea and mandarin oranges are grown on the island and are made into a variety of drinks.

Index